Time To Shine

Clodagh Marie Swanson

Copyright Page

First published 2016

The moral right of Clodagh Swanson to be identified as the author of this work has been asserted in accordance with the Copyright and Related Act, 2000.

©Clodagh Swanson, 2016

www.clodaghswansoncoaching.org

DEDICATION

To Niall, Rory and Niamh: I am proud of you beyond belief. You inspire me every day. To all those who said it could not be done: I did it! I changed my life.
To my family, friends and fellow coaches, I love you all. To my mum who was an inspiration and a friend, and to my brother, I love you.
To all those who I have coached, thank you for allowing me to share in your journey. I honor you. My challenges have allowed me to grow.
Be happy, be strong. Have fun and leave the world a better place.
Live life on life's terms.

God bless x

CONTENTS

My story
Introduction

Acknowledgements

To all those who helped me on my journey many thanks.

MY STORY

My early life was dysfunctional. It was what would be described as a fear-based childhood. My father had a problem with alcohol, and I witnessed drunken behaviour and violence in the home from an early age. I remember many Christmases spent worrying about what was going to happen. I remember sitting in a van as my dad weaved from one side of the road to the other while I screamed for him to stop. He was driving the car or his work van while drunk. I remember every time we heard a knock on the door being frightened in case he broke the door in, which is what happened most times. I remember him breaking in my grandmother's front door. My parents would break up, get back together, and eventually row and break up all over again. I remember one particular Christmas, coming home to find it full of smashed Christmas decorations. The tree was in bits and the house was wrecked. There was a lot more damage done than just to the tree.

Another Christmas, I got roller skates. We were living in a flat, three flights up. My father was putting black and white pudding into my mother's tea to aggravate her. Eventually, and probably still drunk from the night before, he fell asleep. My mother gathered us together and we ran down stairs. Me, my mother and my younger brother ran. Of course, he woke. He ran down the stairs in his socks. I can still see this all so clearly. He bashed my mother's face against a pebble-dash wall until her face was bleeding and her teeth were knocked out. He said if she did not go back upstairs he would choke my brother, and he tightened the jumper around his neck. I ran to every flat, knocking on the doors crying for help. No one answered. We went back upstairs. This was a regular occurrence.

I hated him. Of course, when off the drink he was a lovely man. But sure it was Ireland and it was "the norm". I remember being taken to a pub early one morning and asking where my mother was. He said she was fine and I would see her later. I was less than eight years old at the time. I left, and walked twenty minutes to my grandmother's house. My mother was there, her arm bandaged. He had put all her lovely clothes down the rubbish chute and shut it on her hand. I remember being taken to a psychologist as they could not figure out why I refused to visit my dad. I remember praying that he would die. He eventually did.

Now I realise he was ill and needed help. One night, he got drunk and broke into our house while we were at my grandmother's. He was taken away and about 6 weeks later, he was taken out of the docks, dead. He had been in the water for 5 weeks. Photos were found of me and my brother in his wallet. He was in his early thirties. Drink is a killer. My mother lost the man she loved and we grew up without a dad. Other stuff happened in my childhood that left me feeling guilty, ashamed and dirty but most of us carry hurt and pain; we just need to find a way to deal with it.

All of those memories I lived with for over forty years before I was able to deal with them. I had a very loving extended family and was a happy enough kid. I had panic attacks from age seven up, bit my nails and was nervous and shy. I never felt good enough. I always remember having to ask for the free school books. I always felt like I was not as good as the other girls. The nuns in school did not dispel this. If we were from the working class side of town, we were never going to amount to anything. We were not going to go to college and we were "no good". Well, I proved them wrong. They had such a chance to shape people's lives and they did the opposite. They destroyed the confidence of so many kids.

My son always disliked the Irish educational system. I remember him receiving detention at school on one occasion. The punishment was to write an essay on the Irish education system – he simply wrote, "It is fucked up". The teacher smiled and agreed. I am so proud of him and my other two children who are such strong individuals. School was not kind. It produces sheep and those who are different or special can have a painful time, enduring abuse from students and teachers alike. Teachers reading this: You have the potential to change lives and mould the individual. Do. My daughter speaks of a primary school teacher who everyone loved and she said once, "Mam, he is a legend". How cool it is to have tiny kids in school call you a legend.

I had very good aunts, uncles and cousins and this made a big difference to my life. I loved school but was never able to concentrate. I remember in school one day my history teacher thought I was talking and threw me outside the door. She flung the door open at one point and told me I would not pass history in my exams, so I decided to prove her wrong. Not only did I pass, I got good grades. Another time we were advised to do typing instead of French as we were working class girls and would not be going to college. I did typing for three days and said to myself, 'Stuff that! Who the hell are they to tell me I am not going to college?' I passed my French exam. It was the first year they introduced Oral French and I guessed they would be kind with the marks that year. I was a pretty determined girl.

I started working after school the minute I was sixteen and have not stopped working since, but I do not ever remember being told I was good at anything growing up. I had no confidence at all. I would laugh and joke (the big smile) but behind it all, I was so shy.

After secondary school all I wanted to do was to go to college and study business but I did not get the grades. Even if I did, I could not have afforded to go. My mum was a widow and we had very little money. She had three jobs and I remember her being not only creative with her money but great with a sewing needle and thread. She taught me more than she will ever know. All my children have a creative side which is so wonderful. I worked in retail before going to the UK at the age of twenty one. I worked in the bank and I *hated* it. I had met my husband at sixteen and loved him every day since. I was married at twenty three and had my first son at twenty six. I decided to retrain as a Beauty Therapist and began to teach this after qualifying. We had another son and moved to Holland. At this time, my body crashed and I began to experience severe panic attacks. I could not leave the house or drive the car. There were moments that I would not be able to breath. I thought, "If I go to sleep, I will never wake up".

Eventually, it got better.

I returned from Holland and was offered a teaching job in Dublin. I loved it. I was helping girls learn new skills and I was very happy for a long time. I loved my husband and my boys so much and I really felt my husband was my best friend. Leaving Holland, I had a miscarriage and, later on, a second loss. I had an ectopic pregnancy which was very upsetting and I could have died. It had been at a critical level by the time I had surgery. Luckily, I had a French doctor who managed to keep me together, so to speak, in case I wanted to try for children again. I hoped one day to have a little girl as well as my fantastic boys and eventually I was blessed, after seven years, with the most beautiful girl. My boys were terrific and I was happy. I loved to go to the football and Gaelic matches in the county ground. I loved to support their hobbies and I was very proud of them and even more proud today. They are all artistic, creative individuals with big hearts and they always think of others. I still found life very challenging all the same. I would drink the odd time, but the odd time too much. It was my way of dealing with pain, switching off feelings and hurt. Life was manageable though. I was working and running my own business while doing a four year degree in Training and Education. Every goal I set, I achieved. Whilst teaching beauty therapy, I fell in love with helping people. My students were from quite marginalised areas of Dublin and they had a lot of baggage. They often had seriously damaged home lives and experienced substantial violence, abuse, and, in some cases, severe poverty. I began to look for training to become a life coach. I had realised that I had the ability to look into a person's eyes and could see the pain within them. They may have been telling me that everything was alright, but I could see through the smiles. I remember my husband saying to me, "Why would you want to train as a life coach when your own life is a mess?" I began to see the cracks in that relationship then and there. I got great support for all my dreams from him ... not! At this point my husband had started working with me, and I thought it was going to be great. And when it worked, it worked very well. To be honest though, it ultimately led to too many rows and I really didn't like that. I felt controlled. I was beginning to lose the little bit of confidence I had gathered up myself all over again. At the same time, I worried about my sons who were going to secondary school and the challenges that came with that. I was always a positive person and always optimistic. I achieved so much but I know now why I was constantly achieving and setting goals for myself. I may have been trying to prove to the world that I was good. That I was smart. That I was clever.

I had accumulated so many qualifications by now, but I continued to push myself hard. I had the "I-am-fine" attitude, but I was not fine. I was carrying a lot of pain, hurt and baggage. When I decided to train as a life coach, it was the start of my journey. I began to really look at myself and the world around me, and learned about the other people can have on our lives. Throughout this time I felt my marriage was not working, and we had split up a few times. I always wanted it to work, but I felt small and unsupported. Coaching became my life. I became lonelier and lonelier and kept smiling to the outside world. My relationship was not working and I would, on occasion, drink one or two bottles of wine to switch off the pain in my head and my heart. Of course, this was not a good coping mechanism and, deep down, I realised that it was not the solution to any of my problems. I asked many times if we could work together on the marriage, but nothing changed. I felt guilty over every single thing, coupled with the guilt and shame that I had carried since childhood. I found things really hard to cope with. During all this time I was still working, studying and raising a family. It got bad for me and I was not in a good space. I felt so alone and isolated. 'But I am fine. I am a big girl and I can cope'. That was my mantra since I was a tiny child. I felt that I was not being authentic. I was coaching others and helping them to fix their life … but I was not dealing with my own shit. My life was sometimes too painful.

I took a few weeks off to try to fix myself. I had therapy and counselling and started some really in-depth work on myself. And with that, my personal recovery began. I dealt with each part of my past. I looked at all the anger, hurt and pain. I realised that I was only a child. I was not responsible for most of the things that happened. Happy as it was, a lot of damage had been done. I found my strength during that time and now realise that I am an amazing person. I had been helping others all those years while dealing with my own issues. I had so much to give to the world and I needed to go through all that stuff so that I could better help others. I became involved in the International Coaching Federation and wanted to ideally bring coaching and self-help to individuals at many levels. I continued to study. I applied for a leadership course which was going to cost me back €9,000. It was at one of Ireland's top management institutes. I remember the first day, walking in there and thinking, I should not be here. I am not good enough. I am not smart enough.

I nearly turned away ... but I didn't. I decided to stay and give it a shot. It was the most amazing time of my life.

I found myself during that time, and I proved to myself that I *was* clever and I *was* good enough to be there. I later went on to do a second diploma and this stretched me even further. I had been told I was no good at finance, despite loving it in secondary school, and when it came to the finance section of my management course, I began to panic. I could not breath and I thought, "I cannot do this".

I decided, again, to prove to myself that actually, yes, I could do this. I did all my assignments and projects for the two years without asking for help. I never got anyone to proofread my work as I was afraid I would be judged. I decided to take on the finance challenge and really aim to do well in this one unit. I developed a hunger for finance as a result. I loved it.

On the day my assignment results came in, I was terrified to open the email, and would you believe it, was the highest mark I got in two years! I had won the lottery. I was so proud of myself. I am now working for myself again.

I could no longer work in the business with my husband. I did not want to leave the business but I felt I had no choice. I began to get really fit, both mentally and physically, and was in the gym at least 5 times a week. This really helped me through the rough months, as, at this point, we decided to separate after 23 years of marriage. I was so unhappy it was horrible. I felt I had done everything and it would never be good enough.

But I was also strong now and I didn't want to live half a life anymore. We were separating. As I speak, I am parted from my husband. I am leaving my home and I have started a start a new life.

I am feeling worn out by the emotional pain that comes with all of this but I actually know that I must go through this and that I am doing the right thing. I am so glad that I have had loving friends and family to support me. I am in a very good space and I am enjoying my life. I have never been so financially broke in my life, but I keep focused on my goals. And I achieve them all.

I hand over my day to my silent partner: the big boss man. I ask him to give me a dig out and I am always supported and cared for. I am sent what I need, not what I want. Read this little book and it may just make your journey a little lighter. Life is very challenging right now, but I know I will be fine and so will you.

Remember that the people in your life are sent to help you grow and they need your love. Do remember also that we cannot live ourselves without love, in the same way as a plant will die without sunshine.

Clodagh XXXX

INTRODUCTION

Do you go through each day going through the motions? Without direction? Drifting? As each birthday comes along, you regret that life is passing you by and you are still doing the same old things and not making any progress. What is even worse is you resent people who are living their lives and are achieving. You are happy being unhappy. You are safe in your comfort zone and you will not step out of it. Why do so many people settle for less? What is stopping them? It could be fear, confidence and low self-esteem. You set goals all the time but you fail to keep them. Always giving up easily. This makes you feel even worse about yourself and it is a vicious circle. You become deflated and you begin to have doubts in your ability. I hope in this book you will find a new passion for your life. It may help you to look at your life in a new way. Perhaps it will help you find new ways to approach your life. After all, we only have one. It is precious and you must live it.

In my work as a life coach, I find the main reason why people are unhappy is that they stay in unhappy situations, marriages, relationships or jobs, and they moan about how miserable they are. The number one thing preventing them from going forward is fear. Fear of failure. Or fear of success. You would not think that people are afraid of success but actually they often are. They know that if they succeed this will also bring changes.

There are tools in this book that will help you to reflect. To think about where you are and where you want to be. Tools that will allow you to take small steps, one at a time. They say the way to climb a mountain is to start by taking one small step. Each step brings you closer. They also say the harder the climb, the greater the view from the finishing line. Everything that is worthwhile is often difficult to achieve and will take massive determination and dedication. Let yourself begin now.

I hope you will enjoy this, as much as I will enjoy writing it.

"Here is a test to find whether your mission on earth is finished: If you are alive it isn't". *Richard Bach.*

"Be not simply good: Be good for something". *Henry David Thoreau.*
"Life is not worth living unless in service to others". *Mother Teresa.*

"The ladder of success is never crowded at the top". *Napoleon Hill.*

1. WHERE DO WE START?

Who are you and where are you? What is your life all about? This book aims to get you to look at your life and to evaluate it. Is it going in the right direction? Do you wake each day and groan or sigh before you get out of bed or do you wake energized and ready for the day? Most people moan.

When you are living the life of your dreams or are happy with your life you do not have that heavy feeling in the morning. I know when I am looking forward to my work and the day ahead, I actually wake long before I need to and jump out of bed because I am looking forward to the challenge.

Now before you think, "Is this woman mad thinking like this?" let me tell you that approximately 80% of people are in jobs that they do not like; some even hate their job. This is very, very sad. This affects their home life and all other aspects of their life. When you are happy at work and at home you feel safe. Your health is better and you feel good. You produce more serotonin. When you are unhappy or stressed you produce cortisol which long term is really bad for your body. It lowers the immune system for example. So when you are constantly under pressure, which could be down to issues at home or unhappiness at home or in the workplace, your body stays in a stressed state with a long term devastating effect on the body. Those people that lead happier lives – and that is not necessarily related to the size of their bank balance – they actually live longer. So effectively, if you want to live longer you need to bring a little happiness into your life. I know you can do it.

They say the best things in life are free. For those people who are lucky enough to have a job it is vital that you are happy at work. Why? Because you spend 7 hours or more a day working in your job … That is a very long time to be unhappy – five days a week, possibly multiplied by 48 weeks of the year. I will talk later about happy working environments in the work and career section.

With this little book I want to get you to honestly look at your life and make any improvements or adjustments that will bring you to a new and fulfilling life. You can do it! You have all the resources within you. You just need to go out and get organized and get honest with yourself. Small changes often will result in a huge overall change eventually. In the goal-setting chapter you will learn about how habits are formed and how to develop these new habits. I will help you design a 30-day plan. How do you climb a mountain? You take one small step at a time. There will be no excuses; no "I can't"; only "I will and I can". Why do people never change or why do they not achieve all they can in life? Often they are just plain lazy. It's seen as "too much effort".

Here are some common reasons:

1. **Procrastination.** You keep putting things off. All talk and no action. You are happy to stay unhappy. It

is like sitting in a pile of POO! It stinks, it's an awful place to be, but it's safe and you are used to the smell. Life has not become painful enough for you to change. When it has become painful enough, it may be too late. You could have lost a partner or a business, a loved one may have left you, or you may have health problems because you left something too late. Step out of the poo and smell the roses.

2. **Underestimating what it will take to change. Or you do not know how.** When you decide to make changes you must really investigate and evaluate what it will take to make the changes. You can't run a marathon next week if you only start training today. You need to really have a look at what needs to be done in order to achieve what you want and this might mean many small steps along the way. Get some advice, especially if there are other professionals who can help you. With everything in life there is always someone who has done it before you. Model yourself on them. What does this mean? Coaching originated in the US, and they realised that to become better at something, or to be the best, you had to model yourself on the best. Watch them. Learn from them. Study what they do and then go out and do it. They realised that if we can do this in sport, why not in all aspects of life? And, with that, business coaching was born. But no matter what you are trying to achieve someone else has normally done it before you. Get help! It will cut your time down dramatically if you have someone to guide you. What is it going to

take and who can help you? Ask questions. If you do not know where to start, make a list and find out what you need to find out. It is like baking a cake. Get a cake book, find the recipe and get the ingredients. Get a book or an article on what you want to do. Make a list of your ingredients. What do you need if it is running you are starting? Well, you may need sports clothes, equipment. If it is starting a new business, it may be renting an office or doing a business plan. Then just bake that cake. Do it!

3. **Complaining and moaning**. You spend too much time complaining instead of doing. You do not change how you think about what you *want* to change. You do not change your environment or the people whom you need to be with. They say you should sit with the people you wish to become. You keep doing the same things and expecting to get different results. Like betting ("I will win the next time") or drinking ("Oh one day I will be able to not drink"), or exercise ("one day I will be able to exercise and lose weight"). It is always one day, one day, one day. Today is your "one day".

4. **Distractions**. This is so evident in time management. You make a list at the start of the week of all the things you want to do or achieve and by Monday lunchtime the list has gone out the window. "What happened?" you ask yourself? Well, you got up late which got you right off to a bad start. Then you took on other people's work or stuff and your own got

left behind. So you took the monkey off their back and now you have two on yours. Remember each time you say yes to someone else you say no to yourself. Efficient and effective time management will allow you to achieve more in half the time. Here's a quote: "there is nothing more wasteful than doing something efficiently which should not or need not be done at all". Be strict with your time management and practice strict discipline. Avoid the television, which I was told was 'second-hand living'. Use your time to reach your goals. Prioritise your time and your goals. Too many goals will result in nothing being achieved.

5.   Giving up too easily. It is easier to sit on the couch than to go for a run. "I will start tomorrow". It is easier to eat a take away than cook a healthy meal. It is easier to drink a bottle of wine than have a herbal tea. We all like things that are not good for us and one of the main ways to achieve great things is to make sacrifices. As they say **"ease pays off now, hard work pays off later"**.

They say it takes ten years to become an overnight success. And success is achieved when opportunity meets preparation". Get up off your ass and take action!

Affirm: I will take action!!

Remember! You only fail when you stop trying. Never give up. Here are some famous failures: They said Walt Disney lacked imagination, and he was fired from his job at a newspaper. Abraham Lincoln's fiancé died, he failed at business twice, lost eight elections and had a nervous breakdown. Michael Jordan was dropped from his high school basketball team.

So you cannot give up. It is not always talent that wins, it is often persistence! And practice! Use practice and persistence. I remember once I wanted to work for a specific company. I kept reminding them over email, over the phone, that I was **HERE HERE HERE**. I AM HERE, I STILL HERE! Eventually, I got to work there. You can never take no for an answer.

6. Your goal is not really important to you. You think you want it but do you really? Napoleon Hill in his many books states that you must have a burning desire. You must want it passionately. It must consume you. You need to be sure you really want this goal. How badly do you want it and how far are you willing to go to get what you want? Are you just doing it to please others? Does mum or dad want you to do it? Are you being told you must do this? You will only give a goal your full effort if it is something you really want personally.

7. Your environment. If you want to lose weight and you are surrounded by food, this will not help. If you want to stop smoking and you are in a smoky environment, you need to change the environment. I believe you need to surround yourself with the people that you would like to become. If you would like to be able to dine at the nice restaurants or fine places, then go there! Get dressed up and have a coffee. Feel the experience. This is really important. I took my daughter to a castle for afternoon tea. The luxury of the place, the setting, the service, all these things gave her an opportunity to feel 'worthy' of being there. Put yourself in the zone. How do you feel when you are there? Where do you feel it in your body? When you go home, you can mentally go back there any time you like. It is good to go to where you want to be. Feel it, see it, smell it. And get out of an environment that is not serving you. I was talking to a friend and fellow coach recently she said my old lunch mates no longer are the type of people I need to surround myself with. I need to be around with new people. Of course I can still keep the old lunch buddies for lunch but my new environment must be with the type of people that I want to be working with. Surround yourself with the right people in the right environment. This is vital to success. If you are in the wrong home or work environment then you need to change that. Is it supporting you or is it holding you back? The environment you grew up in can be a force for driving you. You may have grown up in a challenging environment with some poverty or social issues; this may not hold you back it may actually drive you to achieve a better life. I love this and it is a bit like me. I feel when something is really trying to hold you back it is a chance to push forward and really show the world that you can do it. Environment is *vital*.

8. **Limiting beliefs and conditioning**. What you believe will have a massive impact on your actions. Your thoughts create your reality. Perhaps what you have been told growing up "You are no good. You will achieve nothing. You are worthless". This will all affect your success, or lack of it. So you may need to change the way you think. This is not easy but there are many tools and professionals who can help you, including affirmations and self-help books. You have to believe you can do it.

Task 1: What areas of your life are you not satisfied with?

1.

Why?

2.

Why?

3.

Why?

4.

Why?

5.

Why?

Well now it is time to make some **changes**!!!

What do you want? You will never get it if you do not know you want it.

Change the way you think right now. Make a firm commitment to yourself today, *I can, I will*, and be firm in that decision. Begin your new life right now.

I _____ on this day _____ make a firm commitment to change my life for the better.

I totally commit to this.

So what makes up a life as we know it?

- Work
- Family
- College
- Community
- Relationships
- Fun
- Personal Development
- Health
- Fitness
- Hobbies

The list is endless!

Now you can put these on a life wheel as many coaches do, but even just rate them on a scale of 1 (for totally dissatisfied) to 10 (for totally satisfied).

Task 2: Life Wheel

Rate each section from one to ten and then reflect on what areas need improving. If your score is lower than 5, then this area of your life needs work. One section may affect another section so, for example, if you are in poor health, it will affect each other section. If you are unhappy at work, it may lead to ill health. So they interact and affect each other. Your wheel should ideally be well balanced.

Put today's date on this and review it in three months and then again in six months.

Perhaps you are not happy in your relationships or not happy at work. You might have a 5 written down or placed on your wheel. List all the areas that are of concern for you and make a list of things you can do to work on this. Make a plan to work on improving those areas. What are you going to do to change this? What needs to be done?

- List the areas that are of concern for you.
- List who can help you.
- What resources do you have available?
- Give yourself some deadlines.
- What type of life do you want? Ask yourself the following questions:
- What would my ideal life look like?
- Where would I be living?
- What would I be doing?
- What job would I have?
- What would I do in my spare time?
- What type of family would I have?

Key areas of concern (list)

1.
2.
3.
4.
5.

Who can help you? (list)

1.
2.
3.
4.
5.

What would my ideal life look like? (details)

What would my ideal life look like? (*details*)

Where would I be living (*details*)

What would I be doing? (*details*)

What job would I have? (*details*)

Ask yourself all those types of questions. Put it all on a vision board. A vision board is a homemade board with vision for the life you want. It could also be a work vision board, with all your career dreams.

For your vision board, cut out pictures of the places you wish to travel to. The new car you want. Perhaps the house of your dreams. All the things you wish to do. Also stick on pictures of people who inspire you. Who do you most admire in life? Put their picture on there. Small dreams, big dreams it does not matter. Always dream big. "Reach for the moon, even if you miss you may fall among stars".

Put your vision board somewhere where it can be seen many times throughout the day, in the morning and last thing at night. Alternatively, place it near your desk at work. This is a form of visualisation and will keep the pictures and goals fresh in your mind, keeping you focused. Mine is at the end of my bed, on my dressing table. I see it when I wake and when I am heading off to sleep, and guess what? I always achieve those goals. *Always.*

Task 3: Create your vision board!

Buy an artist board or card and cut out pictures of things you want in your life. Put pictures of people who inspire you on it. You might want a holiday spending time enjoying the sun. Maybe you would like a new fitter and healthier body. Whatever you dream of!

A goal book is another great idea. There is no good in having goals if they are not written down. The purpose of goals is to give you direction. They are what you need to be concentrating your time on. "Why", I hear you say? When you write them down clearly you have much more of a chance of them coming to fruition.

- Goals help you to focus on what is really important.
- Goals can provide direction if you are working as a team.
- Helps you to avoid wasting time on goals which are not important or critical to you.
- Goals should motivate you.

Some goals will be short term while others long term. When the goal is big, you may have to set many smaller goals to help you achieve the big goal. Some goals are classed as 'critical' while others are classed as 'enabling'. Enabling goals may support your critical goals.

Goals also need to have a deadline and you need a plan. A page should be allocated for each goal. Write one goal on each page, with a date for its achievement. A goal book should be a lovely, beautiful book. One that you are happy to look at! I will explain how to set your goals properly later on but for now, start dreaming.

Remember a goal is only a dream with a deadline. Do not let anyone steal or put you off your goals. They are dream stealers. Believe in yourself and go for it. There is a full chapter on goal setting later on.

Task 4: Creating your goal book.

- Create a page for each goal.
- What is the reason why you want that goal?
- Who can help you achieve it and what resources are available to you?
- What you will gain from achieving the goal?
- What will it cost you, what will be the disadvantages of gaining the goal?
- When you achieve it cross it off – write 'achieved, well done'.

Next what do we want to change?

The Change Table. (*You can include this in your goal book*)

This is just a guide you can design your own list.

Now after having a look at the things you want to change in your life and the things you wish to make better, (make sure you have a list already made), let us look at the reasons why we do not live our life to the full. We shall begin with the top barrier of all to progression.

2. FEAR

What are you afraid of?

"Fear knocked on the door, faith answered it, and there was no one there".

"Fear is a dark room where negatives are made". This must be one of my favourite quotes. I was sitting on a battered old bus driving through Delhi in India and I saw this painted on a wall and I thought, "I love that".

Fear is not tangible. You cannot buy a bucket of fear. You cannot see it. You cannot touch it. It is an emotional state. The one thing about emotional states is that you can actually change your emotional state in as little time as it takes to blink. In surveys the most common types of fears found were, ghosts, evil spirits, snakes, spiders, heights, closed spaces, tunnels, failure, social rejection, public speaking, examinations, bridges, and cockroaches. But the number one fear above all is public speaking. Can you imagine! I have been training for 20 years and I still often feel physically ill before a talk or lecture, especially if it is important or if there are people present whom I need to impress. Wow! It is a very normal occurrence.

Task 5: Identify your top ten fears! And explain why.

(*List all ten*)

In one survey study undertaken on people's fears, these were the top ten:

1. Fear of failure
2. Death
3. Rejection
4. Ridicule
5. Loneliness
6. Misery
7. Disappointment
8. Pain
9. The unknown
10. Loss of freedom

There are different types of fear. Fear of things that will definitely happen, and fear of things that may never happen. Most times, we are afraid of things that may never happen. Often we project into the future. People are constantly thinking: 'What if this happens? What if that happens? What if I ask her out and she says no? What if I ask her out and she says yes? What if I do not get the job? What if I do not get an interview?

That is a lot of what ifs. People are so intent on thinking of the future and dwelling on the past that they do not enjoy the day they are in. I find I do this myself but I am working on changing this. Planning for the future is one thing but worrying about it is another. *The Power of Now* by Eckhart Tolle is an excellent book on practicing just being in the now.

Yoga and meditation also help you to focus on the present and the notion of the "now".

People always fear the worst. It is actually a mind-set. They go straight to negative mode. They are always looking at the half empty glass instead of the half full glass. Fear is good, to some extent. Fear protects us from danger and warns us of impending dangerous situations. We need fear at certain times. The fight or flight mechanism in our body warns us of danger and we either fight or flight. What actually happens to the body when the fight or flight mechanism occurs?

- Heart rate increases
- Lung action is accelerated
- Blood loss from skin resulting in a pale color the blood vessels constrict
- Inhibition of the digestive functions, digestion slows down or stops
- Liberation of fat and glucose to aid muscular action supplying the muscles with energy. So we can run away.
- Dilation of the blood vessels in muscles
- Dilation of the pupils
- Relaxed bladder
- Tunnel vision
- Shaking

All of the above are normal reactions to stress and the body will return to normal once the fright or danger has passed. However, when someone is suffering long-term under stress, or in continually stressful situations, their body suffers as a result. The immune system suffers and the body becomes susceptible to illness and disease. The long-term production of steroids greatly affects the body. (See the section on stress management for guidelines on how to deal with stress.) Fear is a normal reaction to situations.

So fear is good. Fear before examinations or before interviews is more like anxiety or apprehension, but it is good fear. It helps you to perform better if you are a little afraid, so they say. But the main problem is when fear actually starts to interfere with your life. When it stops you from going out and from doing things you may actually want to do. People who suffer from anxiety attacks or panic attacks know exactly what I am talking about. As a child I had panic attacks and later, when I was twenty-six, this happened again. I was driving along a dual carriageway with a ten-week old baby in the car seat and panic came over me. I had to stop the car and get out to breath. I tried to park and stopped in an underground car park where I panicked again. I did not go into car parks for years after this attack, because each time I did I got that panic again. Now this is fear of absolutely nothing. This is what makes it so frightening. I had nothing to be afraid of. Many people suffer from panic attacks and they may need to speak to their doctor. Quite often it is the body's way of telling you to slow down, that you're exhausted or not well. You may be under so much pressure and not know it. This could be an accumulation of subconscious issues and can all result in panic attacks. You are not losing your mind – you may just be over tired or exhausted. Seek medical help. Quite often however, doctors will have a prescription written for antidepressants or tranquillizers as it is a quick fix to get you out of the surgery. I found the best thing for me was acupuncture, exercise and just actually talking to myself and saying, right the panic will be gone soon. Just wait and it will go away. If you take medication you are not directly dealing with the real problem. You are just dealing with the symptoms. Until you look at the underlying issues, the problem and their causes, it will never go away. Do seek medical help, however, as sometimes there may be a chemical deficiency in the brain or the body causing the panic, as can happen with a thyroid disorder.

Anxiety. Feeling apprehensive the odd time is alright but when it is continuous and for no reason you may be suffering from anxiety. The symptoms of this are similar to what is known as your 'fight or flight' reaction, but with anxiety it can come out of nowhere and for no reason. Alternatively, it may be related to something that upset you in the past and when you meet that thing or similar in the future you become anxious.

Common physical symptoms of anxiety include:

- Pounding heart
- Sweating
- Stomach upset or dizziness

- Frequent urination or diarrhoea
- Shortness of breath
- Tremors
- Muscle tension
- Headache
- Fatigue
- Insomnia

In addition to the primary symptoms of irrational and excessive fear and worry, other common emotional symptoms of anxiety include:

- Feelings of apprehension or dread
- Poor concentration
- Feeling tense and jumpy
- Anticipating the worst
- Irritability
- Restlessness
- Watching for signs of danger
- Feeling like your mind's gone blank

You might not even know what that issue or concern is but in general, if people have suffered some trauma or distress then even the smallest thing can push them too far.

How to deal with anxiety:

We all worry from time to time but continuous anxiety is too stressful for our system and we need to take care of ourselves.

- Do you make time each day for relaxation and fun?
- Are you getting the emotional support you need? A lady once said to me "Clodagh what petrol station do you pull into to get refuelled?" I thought this was a good analogy.
- Are you taking care of your body?
- Are you overloaded with responsibilities?
- Write down what is worrying you and share your worries.
- Do you ask for help when you need it?
- Write up some affirmations to help you through the panic.
- Make sure you rest even if you cannot sleep. A rest will do you just as much good.

I would personally recommend a coach or someone to talk to. Try to look at what is bugging you. Eventually you will get to the bottom of it. I would also recommend natural therapies such as Bach Flower remedies, which can be very good in helping you deal with stress, fear and anxiety. Rescue Remedy is used by many people. A coach or counsellor will help you explore your worries or fears. I have found that you can heal your fear and your anxiety by realising that the panic will pass. Go with it. Ride the wave, it will pass. Take deep breaths and keep saying "I will be fine, I will be fine".

People have got through some horrific things or situations in life and they just keep on going. Please do get professional help with your panic attacks or your fears. It is a lonely place to be but there is help out there. Gently exercise or a walk will also help initially it will also calm you down. Yoga and breathing exercises will really benefit you. Back to fear. Panic may be due to something that happened to you in the past and you may be able to work through this with various tools and the help of experts. Neuro-Linguistic Programming (NLP) is a great tool for going back to traumatic events and working through them.

Contact the Irish Association of NLP or get a list of NLP practitioners in the phone book or online. 'Time Line' is a technique used by NLP experts which you could explore, and many other similar tools are available, including hypnotherapy.

When you have an actual fear or phobia of something again you can work with a coach or professional to deal with it. Spiders, lifts or flying are common fears. This fear can be about control as opposed to lifts or planes. Sometimes the things you think you are afraid of are not actually the real cause. When you look at it in detail and break it down it may be a different cause. For now, I will just talk about everyday fear.

These are the simple things that stop you from doing what you want to do or what you need to do.

As we mentioned earlier, there are two main types of fear: fear of things that will actually happen; and fear about things that may never happen.

Things that will happen:

- You will get older
- You will die
- You will become ill at some point
- You will retire
- You will lose a friend or loved one
- Your children will grow and leave home
- Your life will change
- You may have a fear of making the wrong decision
- Fear of loneliness
- Fear of loss of freedom
- Fear of the unknown

All of these things happen naturally and there is nothing you can do about them. So why do you worry about them? You are wasting an awful amount of energy on things that you cannot control. What happens is that people become wrapped up in their thoughts. What will I do when I get older? How will I cope? What if, What if. What you could actually do is make a list of all your worries. A worry book is good for this. Every time you have a worry, write it down. Ask yourself this, what is the worst thing that could happen? What are the potential options available to me? Who can help me? Then park it. Do not give it more time than is necessary.

When you write things down and look at it on paper, often the power is taken out of it.

The main types of fears we live with on a daily basis, however, are about things that may never happen. What if I ask her out and she laughs at me and she says no. What if I do not get an interview? Things are bad at work, what if I lose my job? Let's reframe those two things now.

What if she says no?

Well you have a 50% chance that she may say yes. They are good odds. If I was backing a horse, they would be very good odds. You just have to be positive. Well sure you have nothing to lose and everything to gain. You must think positive. Nothing ventured, nothing gained.

Things are bad at work, what if I lose my job?

It could be a blessing in disguise. It may give you time to look at what is really important in your life. Ask yourself, "What would I really like to do with my life? What skills do I have and what would I like to spend the rest of my life doing?" When someone loses a job they have the perfect opportunity to look at options available to them. 80% of people are said to be in work that they do not like. What a waste of a life. Going into work every day and going through the motions, wishing they were somewhere else. So if you lose your job you may be losing a job and gaining a life. When you lose your job you could visit a career coach. They will go through your skills, passions and identify with you a plan to achieve what you really want. Remember every problem comes with a gift. A career coach will help you make plans for the future and set some new goals.

Some fears are more about the ego and status:

- Fear of success
- Fear of failure
- Fear of criticism
- Fear of not being important
- Fear of not being loved
- Fear of not being good enough
- Fear of poverty
- Fear of rejection
- Fear of not being liked

The worst thing about these fears is that they impact not just one area of your life, but many areas. If you are afraid of failure it will stop you from doing so much. You will not go for opportunities you are afraid that you will fail. Fear of rejection will prevent you from loving and gaining love. People are afraid to step out of their comfort zone. They are afraid to risk being hurt. They are not happy at all but they stay there often for the rest of their life. They are afraid to stay, afraid to go. When I am coaching a client and they use the term cannot, I challenge them. Oh boy do I challenge them! Why can't you?

Let's take an example:

Client: I hate my job but I cannot leave.
Coach: Why can you not leave?
Client: I can't.
Coach: Why not?
Client: I have a wife and children to look after.
Coach: Have you looked at other jobs?
Client: There is no point. (Assumption)
Coach: Why not?
Client: Who would give me a job now at my age? (Assumption)
Coach: Why would they not give you a job? Are you not a good worker?
Client: I am a good worker but I am too old. (Negative Self-Belief)
Coach: Who said you are too old?
Client: Well ... nobody.
Coach: Well, on what grounds do you think that they would think you are too old?
Client: Well ... (No answer).
Coach: Right, let's go back over this. You do not like your job, and you do not think that you can leave because no one will give you a job because you are too old. Have you (A) tried to get a job or (B) been told that you were too old?

Client: Well, no I have not tried to get a job and nobody told me I was old but ... (*Excuses, excuses, excuses*).

So I challenge the client to look at their options. Right, you said you cannot get a job but you have not even tried. Well, do you not think that if you tried, you would then know whether or not it was actually possible? You will not know until you try.

Often the client will be reluctant but you can work with them to at least explore their options. If plan A does not work, try plan B. If plan B does not work, try plan C, and so on. Often the fear in our own mind is just that: it is only in our *own* mind.

Now if this client had been made redundant at short notice, he would find he was given no choice and would be thrown in at the deep end. He would have to cope.

The problem is that most people just think, think, think. Stop thinking and start living, start trying, and remember you only fail when you stop trying.

How to deal with fear:

Share your worry. Tell someone that you are actually afraid. Often people will have some of the same fears as you. Recognise that everyone will be afraid at some point.

Speak to someone about your fear: a coach or counsellor or even a best friend or family member.

Explore where you are feeling the fear in your body and try to let it go. Take some deep breaths. Write your fear or worry down and burn it or shred it. Get it out of your head and say good bye to it if you can. Try and understand your fear a little better.

Try and come up with a strategy for the fear. What will I do if this fear comes up again? Work with a coach and devise a routine for dealing with fear.

Use visualisation techniques to see yourself as a strong, calm individual. There are courses you can undertake for this.

Face your fear and take the power out of it. How many times were you afraid to do something but you really wanted to do it? The 'want' to do something was greater than the 'fear', in the end. If you give into fear you may miss some of the most amazing experiences of your life. You must just do it. Face your fear and do it. With fear people just think, "I just will not be able to handle it". You do not know what you can handle until it presents itself to you. When you analyse it, what is really stopping you? Be honest. They say people are like tea bags: you do not know how strong they are until they get into hot water!

What is stopping you?

Nothing!

So if there is nothing stopping you why don't you just do it?

You have everything to gain and nothing to lose.

Have a think about the following: The fear will never go away if you let it stay. Get rid of it. Do something about it. Talk to someone who specialises in the area there are some great techniques out there such as

NLP, Cognitive Behavioural Therapy (CBT) and Hypnotherapy. Remember that others are also in fear. You are not alone. A lot of fear comes down to our beliefs and our conditioning. Self-sabotage is very common and again we have many techniques to deal with these. (See later chapters on this subject). When you are tired you will never feel powerful or strong enough to deal with what life throws at you. Things will always look worse than they are. Just realise that you are tired and that when you are feeling a little bit better, things will not seem so bad. You will not be as frightened. Getting plenty of rest will always allow you to feel better. Panic attacks quite often hit you when you are tired or hungry with low sugar levels.

Conditioning

When you were a child you were afraid of nothing! You climbed trees and played happily. Your parents, however, told you to be careful to mind yourself. They passed their fears onto you. "Don't do that, you might hurt yourself". The teachers in school made you conform. Wouldn't it be wonderful to be a child again? Conditioning has a lot to do with fear. If you are told as a child that you are no good, that you will never amount to anything, how do you think your confidence will be? Low if not non-existent. If you are told something long enough you will begin to believe it. If you are told you're useless or ugly you will not think any different. Parents and teachers have such an opportunity to develop confidence in individuals.

They put your dreams down. Never listen to them. It is very hard when you have years of people telling you that you can't do it. You will have to reprogram yourself. You will be able to slowly change the way you feel and think but it will take time.

With fear just say, "I can do this, I will do this, I can achieve great things". Change your mind-set. It can be done. Remember though, if it takes you one hundred feet to get into the forest, it will take you one hundred feet to get out.

Quotes on Fear:

- "Fear is a dark room where negatives are made." *(unattributed)*
- "Fears are nothing more than a state of mind." *(unattributed)*
- "Thinking will not overcome fear but action will." *(W. Clement Stone)*
- "So many fail because they don't get started. They don't go. They fail to begin." *(W. Clement Stone)*

3. NEGATIVE TALK AND LIMITING BELIEFS

What are limiting beliefs? When you have a limiting belief you cannot see things as they really are. Your view is distorted. What you believe, someone else may not see the same way. Limiting beliefs will prevent you from living a truly rich life. They will hold you back. Negative thinking will also hold you back.

Listen to yourself today: "Oh God, I do not want to get up! I am so tired. How can I face another day? It is going to rain today. I will never get all my work done. I will run out of time. Oh, more bills arrived in the post. How will I ever pay them? Life is hard, God I am sick of this! What's the point?"

Well, that is really going to get you off to a good start isn't it? If you are in a negative frame of mind you will stay in a negative frame of mind. Negative people are not nice to be around. In fact they completely drain your energy. They are like parasites. You will feel totally exhausted by the time you are finished. They always look at the dark side of things. I am living in Ireland and, while we are one of the friendliest nations, boy do we have a negative attitude a lot of the time. It could be the most sunny day and someone will turn around and say, "ah yeah, but it's going to rain on Friday".

Let us look at some of the negative self-talk or limiting self-beliefs we have:

- I am too old
- I am too stupid
- I am not clever enough
- I am not good enough
- I would never get that job. There is always someone better than me.
- I do not have the qualifications
- There is no point looking for a job there are none
- I am not pretty enough or handsome enough
- I can't do it I do not have enough money

These are both negative thoughts and limiting beliefs. When you say them to yourself, if you feel the negativity in your abdominal area, this is a limiting belief.

These are only a few small ones. If you speak constantly in the negative mode you will view all things negatively. Try putting an elastic band on your wrist and pulling that elastic band each time you hear yourself say a negative phrase relating to you or your life. Another method I use is when I put myself down (and I can be very hard on myself), I think of an ugly hag sitting on my shoulder and each time she comes out I tell her to get back in her box and stay there. Do not entertain her. Find a method for yourself. Affirmations are a good way to do this. Your mind will listen subconsciously to what it is told. There is a lot being said these days about positive thinking and affirmations, but they really do work. You have to recondition your mind to firmly believe. Even if you do not believe yourself at the start – *try it.*

Negative thinking can have a very damaging effect on you and your future success. It is very important that you monitor it.

Do you find that you do not attempt to do things because of what others will say or how they will react?

Do you not contribute to discussions or conversations because you feel inadequate in some way?

Do you avoid conflict and say yes to things you wish you could say no to?

Do you let others take control of situations?

A lot of this is because of negative self-talk and limiting beliefs.

Keep a log for a week of each time you feel you have a negative thought or belief about yourself.

Task 6: Limiting Beliefs Check-list

- Thought – "the belief"

- Where?

- When?

- Who?

- How do I feel?

- Where in my body do I feel it?

Monitor it and then reflect on the actual reality of it.

Reduce negative thinking.

I was told when I had a negative thought to say to myself – "Cancel, Cancel, Cancel". Do not go there!

Stand up and move out of the space you are in. This will break that train of thought.

Keep a worry book or worry list. This can be especially helpful at night time when you are worried and full of often negative thoughts such as "I can't do that. I will not get through all that tomorrow. I will never get it all done". Spend a few minutes clearing your mind each night prior to getting into bed. Write a worry list on a sheet of paper or put it into your worry book and this means it is out of your head and on paper. It will do two things for you:

1. Reduce the amount of clutter in your head.
2. Take the power out of the thoughts and leave them down on paper.

What are limiting beliefs?

A limiting belief is a belief you have about yourself, your life or your situation. The limiting part means that the belief you have about yourself limits you and your progress. These limiting beliefs may have been built over many years often from childhood. Adults, parents, teachers and so on may have conditioned you to think in certain ways about yourself. You can change all that.

Example:

I am not clever enough – this could be changed to the following affirmation:
'I am a bright and clever individual who is very capable'.

Task 7: Identify and list all your current limiting beliefs:

Beliefs (list five)

What you can change them to (list five)

Work on these everyday a few times a day until they are embedded in your mind.

Negative thinking

Each morning it is a good idea to start the day by being thankful for all the good things in your life. **The Attitude of Gratitude.** Your health, family, friends, your ability to work, your ability to walk, your sight, your home, your lovely children, and on and on. Be grateful for all you have when other individuals may have nothing. You have a home, a car, food; some have nothing.

Another fun thing to do is to think as you wake, Think: what amazing things will happen today? I have no idea what the day will bring! Is that not terrific in itself? Imagine that none of know what is waiting for us, one massive surprise!

Who will I meet? What will I learn? It is exciting.

Get up early enough to be calm and to start the day well. I find a good breakfast and exercise before I hit the office sets me up for the day. If I go to the gym before work I get so much more done. I used to hate exercise but once I got used to it, I could not live without it and my life got so much better.

If driving to work, try to think positive thoughts each time you are stuck in traffic or the car is stopped. I will win that contract! I am a great success! I am delighted to be alive. Positive! Positive! Positive!

Start the day positive. Remember that no matter what goes wrong, and things will go wrong, you can start your day again at any minute of any hour. It is as simple as that.

Ways to deal with negative thoughts and limiting beliefs:

Change your thought processes, like so:

4. Belief Systems and Values

What are belief systems? This is your view of the world. How you view things, how you see things. Our beliefs are set over many, many years. As a child you are conditioned and led by adults, your friends, peers and teachers. You often believe what they say without question. However they are passing on their beliefs to you. As you grow older you may start to question those beliefs. You may go your own way. Often this happens with religion, you grow up with one set of religious beliefs but later in life you question and change your beliefs. Not only may one person be affected but a whole nation or indeed the whole world may change a set of beliefs due to an incident. Look what happened in the world when Hitler decided to kill millions of Jews because of his own beliefs. People followed him they changed their belief systems. Our belief systems do not always serve us well. We often need to change them. We are easily led. Hitler conditioned a whole country and race to believe him. What do you believe? And are those beliefs serving you well or causing obstacles in your life?

Our beliefs affect how we operate in the world around us. Therefore it is imperative that our beliefs serve us well. If we have beliefs which are negative, which discriminate or cause a problem to others they do not serve us well and will often lead to trouble, hurt and pain not just for others but also pain for ourselves. Mainly our beliefs are about how we see our self. In most cases our beliefs are negative beliefs. We have negative beliefs about our self.

Those negative beliefs will hold us back from living the life we deserve to live. Negative beliefs may appear something like this:

- Irish people drink too much.
- German people are always on time.
- Children should be seen and not heard.
- Unemployed people are just lazy.
- Women should stay at home and mind the children.
- Men are the breadwinners.

The list is endless. Often comments made by others will result in having a very long lasting impact on our self-worth and self-belief. Parents are very guilty of doing this to children and teenagers.

'Where are you going dressed like that? Sure who will be looking at you?'

This is a typical Irish saying from a parent, after spending hours getting ready for a night out! What a confidence killer!

You must examine the way you look at life, and how your belief systems are currently functioning. Are there any that you need to deal with and rectify? Identify your main beliefs and clarify which ones serve you well and which ones do not serve you at all. If they do not serve you well change them or get rid of them.

Task 8: Belief systems. Change the negative to positive

Current beliefs (list five):

New beliefs (list five):

In NLP there are techniques you can use to work on your limiting beliefs. You go through the limiting belief and work through the feelings associated with them, and then you swap them with the positive beliefs or a belief that you firmly believe in. See an NLP practitioner for more information this.

Often people will be conditioned over a long period of time. Perhaps, you are in a bad or controlling relationship. You are being told you're no good, you are criticised, and you are belittled. You feel worthless and this eventually wears you down and you believe it. Try and get professional help from a coach or a counsellor, perhaps some NLP. You can change the way you think and blossom into the new and strong person that is inside. The thing about beliefs is that you can change how you think in an instant. Instantly it is that quick.

Values

Our values are very important as to how we play the
game of life. What is important to you? What means
the most to you? How do you live out your values?
Often we say we value something but in reality we are
not living it. An example of this would be someone
who stays at work night and day says they are doing it
for their family. But in reality they never see or spend
time with their family so they are not living the value.
Someone might say they value their health, but they
get no exercise, they smoke have a poor diet and they
drink too much. Let's have a look at your values. What
do you value?

Task 9: Core Values

Examples of core values could be: money, success, career, family, your home, security, being liked or loved, having a sense of purpose, a loving relationship, fun and joy in your life. What do you value? What is important to you? What really matters to you?

Jot down the top ten things that matter to you more than anything else in the world. Keep a separate list for your career values if you wish, or combine the two. What are your core values as a person?

List your ten core values:

Ask yourself – what people are most important to me?

What way do I want to spend the rest of my life?

When I pass on what would I like to leave behind, how do I want people to remember me?

What do I like to share with others?

What is calling me in life? What do I get a calling to do but I am not pursuing?

What are the things that I would love to dearly do?

What am I passionate about?

You also need to ask yourself what causes you hurt, pain or distress. What makes you sad? How can you achieve what you want and avoid what you do not want?

Ask yourself all those questions.

Now, are you actually living life according to those values or are you saying one thing and doing something else? We all do this to an extent.
Often you will hear a man say "I am working all the hours God sends to feed and look after my family". But after doing an 80-hour week they do not see or spend any time with that family. They are not living their life according to their values.

Values for your career are also very important as you will often spend seven hours a day in work and the values you have in your chosen career will either support you or cause problems in your working life. What are your top career values?

Task 10: What are your career values?

Job satisfaction, respect, rewards, financial wages, recognition, promotion, honesty, integrity, and so on.

(*List your top ten career values*):

Does your current job or career meet your career values? If honesty is one of your values and your boss wants you to sell in a dishonest manner, can you live with that? You must be aligned with your values or you will suffer. Eventually there will be inner turmoil. Conflict may arise within you. There may be also external conflict within the workplace and even in the home. You may be asked to do something which is not in line with your values. You are asked to work late every night when you want to be with your young family. You may be asked to be dishonest or disloyal. When you are doing this you are not able to perform to the best of your ability and you feel guilt. Eventually this will wear you down. Businesses will have no problem asking you to dismiss your beliefs or values bottom line is the bottom line. They do not care as long as the job is done. Do you really want to work for a company like this? When deciding on your career or job do a check, does it meet with your own personal career and personal values? If not move on! You need to be happy within yourself doing what is right for you.

For each value you select write out a statement to reinforce that value.

Value Statement

For example, if one of your values is health you could write:
I will eat a balanced diet daily, avoid toxins and get plenty of rest.
I will work out three times a week and walk once a week. I will avoid stress.
If financial security is a value you could write something like this, I shall spend wisely and save weekly. I shall invest in a pension and monitor my finances weekly. I shall secure my final mortgage payment before I am sixty.

Roles in life

Also look at your roles in life. What roles do you have and what roles do you play? Are you giving each role the time required or are some of your roles suffering? Examine them in detail.
You might be a mother, sister, daughter, friend, neighbour, wife, teacher, Aunt. How do you balance all of these roles and are any suffering?
Look at them over the past week. How much time did you spend in each role?

Roles - My Examples:

- Mother
- Sister
- Daughter
- Wife
- Aunt
- Neighbour
- Friend
- Community Leader
- Scout Leader
- Coach

Task 11: Roles

What roles do you fulfil? (*List your top five*)

Did you allocate time for each role this past week?
(*List a role you fulfilled each day of last week*)

You are so busy sometimes just living, working and getting the kids to school that your day and week is gone and there is no time for the important roles in our life, such as mother, wife and daughter. We say, 'Oh, I will call to my mother tomorrow', and tomorrow never comes. I will take my husband somewhere nice next week and next week never comes. Look at what people are important in your life before it is too late.

You also need to value you!

Spend time on you, time out, time to relax, time to breath, time to just be. I find this so hard. I never sit down, I can't and I find that I have to work really hard at down time, but again this is my makeup. I am an activist. So it is difficult for me to be still but I am aware of that and now I can try to do something about it. Awareness is everything. If you are not aware of something, of what you are doing or saying how you expect to change. Awareness comes first. Take time for you. Value yourself and your time. Make time for yourself. You are no good to others if you are not well and not in good mental space. Like on an aircraft you put the oxygen mask on you first before you help others. A doctor will always say to a mother, look after you first and then the child. It makes good sense.

Each value needs a value statement to make it clear what and how you will enforce and monitor those values.

Finally place your values in order of importance. Health might come first and money last. It depends on you but remember if you are not well all the money in the world is no good to you.

Your values may change many times over your lifetime. That is alright. Just ensure you are living according to your values.

Quotes on Love:

- "Before you were conceived I wanted you, before you were born I loved you, before you were here an hour I would die for you. This is the miracle of love." *(Maureen Hawkins)*
- "God cannot be everywhere so he made mothers." *(Arab Proverb)*
- "We make a living by what we get paid for but we make a life by what we give." *(Winston Churchill)*

5. DEALING WITH CHANGE

Everyone will face change in their life. The one thing about change is that it is consistent. People, businesses and large corporations all live through change. Many hide their head in the sand and do not deal with the eminent changes. They hope the changes will go away or indeed the problem or situation will fade into the darkness. Not so. They should embrace change. We have change all through our life. Starting with childhood, teenager, adult, and pensioner, that is life. With each change come good and bad times, happy times and difficult times. Why do people hate change so much? Fear!

Fear is actually not tangible. You cannot buy a bucket of fear. Fear of change is what keeps many people from moving forward in their life. Fear of taking a chance on love. Fear of making a fool of yourself. Fear of letting others seeing our true feelings. How many times have you wanted to make a change in your life but through fear you held back. Change comes with some of the happiest times in our life, marriage, a new house, a new baby, a new job, promotion.

But these times of change can also be a time of great stress and difficulty. It is your reaction to change that is important. The famous book *Who Moved my Cheese?* is a brilliant book to read. It was written by Spencer Johnson. It is about some little mice and someone moved their cheese. They kept going around in circles looking for the cheese. But the mice never made progress. Instead of looking for the old cheese, they should have been sourcing new cheese. This is like us facing a problem and staying in the problem. Instead we should be looking for and finding a solution. If you stay in the situation mentally, then you will stay there physically. Instead live in the solution.

Anyway back to change. If you understand that change is part of life and it will always be then you can begin to work with change and improve your life dramatically. Many people have gone through some very traumatic life changing events, which at the time they thought they would never be able to live with and look at the results. In some cases this changed the world. I am sure Nelson Mandela was not happy with the change in his living arrangements when he arrived on Robin Island, but he took this change and he changed, not only his life, but the life of South Africans for generations to come. Whenever you are faced with a change look at the change and try to view it with potential. They say that every problem comes with a gift. I really believe it does. They look for the golden nuggets hidden within. What good can come of this? How can I turn this around? The problem with most people is they go straight into negative mode. It's terrible, it is a disaster. They think they will never get over it. But, even recently, I have had to say to myself: 'Come on. Things will get better.' I cannot tell you how many times in life something terrible happened and I thought it was the end of the world. Was it? Of course it was not. If you understand change a little better then perhaps you will work with it instead of against it. Let us look at the four 'C's of change.

The 4 'C's of Change

1 – *Comfort zone.* It is safe and we will not step outside the box. We live life on auto pilot. We are often unhappy in the comfort zone but we do not change. It is easier to stay miserable, often for years of in fact for our whole life. We often blame others for us being unhappy. We are the captain of our ship. Only we can steer the ship in a new direction. We often turn to drink, smoking, drugs, retail therapy, chocolate, sex, exercise or other methods of distraction. We will do whatever makes us feel happy. But long term we still feel restless and unhappy. We are not happy but we do not change. I call this the circle of poo! It is shit in here. It stinks but we stay. It is terrible. But we are afraid to step outside and smell the roses.

2 – *The Challenge Zone.* We begin to look at our self or our situation? What can we do to fix this? I cannot live like this any longer, I have had enough. We struggle with fear, and anxiety, doubts and confusion. We often have two voices in our head, you can and you can't. We really need to dig deep to find the strength to make the changes we know we must make. In our heart we know that we need to change. A coach can help you here. Clarify your goals, and dreams, ask what is holding you back. When you make one small change you will not notice it. Make a

small change each week and you will see a huge change eventually. Think of the gym. You start to go and you're half dead on the treadmill. Each day you slog and wear yourself out. Each day you get stronger and stronger mentally and physically. And before you know it you look like a god or goddess. Belief me you do. All those extra pounds are gone. It did not happen overnight. It was a long difficult process. But each small step brought the rewards. Big rewards! To climb a mountain you start with one small step and you start with the view of the top of the mountain. Keep looking at where you are headed. Not where you are, keeping looking at the end. Keep looking at the finishing line.

3 – *Creative Zone*. You begin to look at your options. What can I do? How can I improve this? You may get help and decide to make a plan. How can I deal with this change to move into the future? Who can help me? What resources do I have myself? Set your goal plan and your desired outcomes. Allocate deadlines and targets. With the aid of a coach you will be able to see how your goals or dreams can be transformed into reality. Remember a dream is only a goal with a deadline!

It's your time ...

So turn your 'dreams' into 'how's and your 'one day's into 'now's.

4 – *Content Zone*. After all our hard work in the mental gym working out we can now see real results. We are more confident, we have achieved great things. We have taken many steps towards a better life, a happier

life. We have firstly met each change and challenge and we have faced it, dealt with it and worked through it. We are now more confident in our ability. With each small achievement we gain new confidence. Our self-esteem and belief in our self grows. When you have a doubting voice in your head, this self-limiting voice will stop you from achieving. Think of it as an ugly person, I think of it as an old hag, with warts, and a hairy face, and each time it pops up I tell it to get out of my space. I tell it to get back into the box. I do not entertain it and its negative attitude. Another thing to do is anytime you have a negative thought about yourself wear an elastic band and pull it each time you think a negative thought, or a limiting belief comes up. Finally the way you react to change will have a large impact on your outcome.

E+R=O   **Event** plus **response** equals **outcome**.

If you meet a change and you fight it you are likely to fight it forever. It may eat you up or you may decide to move on (different response) and you find your get a better outcome.

There are five steps –

- Pre contemplation – this is before you even start thinking of making a change.
- Contemplation – you begin to think about change.
- Preparation – You start changing your behaviour.
- Action – Change of behaviour consistently.

- Maintenance – You maintain these changes for over six months.

Change is part of life. However people quite often do not change until things get really painful. They need to be motivated to change. In the business world they call it your burning platform. There must be an urgent important need for drastic action. Often we only change when we have lost. Some of us have had a heart attack, had a melt-down, lost a loved one. Make those changes now before it is too late. Always go with the heart. The times I have gone with my gut and my heart I have always been ok. Logic will often hold you back, keep you safe. Safe is boring. When I started this book, I never in a million years realised what changes were ahead of me. I have now experienced separation, moving to a different home, to a different place and rebuilding my business. It has been so challenging and there were really days when I thought I cannot hang on any longer. This is all too much. But I had to go through all of it. Someone once said that the elevator sometimes needs to go down before it can go up. I just kept believing and trusting that it would all work out. I had faith. Sometimes that faith was, in fact, all I had. I kept going when I wanted to quit. I had a coach friend who said, "Clodagh, when you get to the end of your rope, tie a knot in it and hang on". Thanks Al. So many times I had to hang on to that rope in the past year. Without change we stay the same. Life is a process of growth and adventure and sometimes we hit storms but there is always a sunny day eventually. And I found a lovely piece one day that said. When we have a storm it is just nature's way of dealing with the pressure. It is like our storms. There is always light after dark. The tide always comes in again and as my son Rory said. You can't have a rainbow without a little rain.

Embrace change. You can change or stay the same.

Task 12: Change

What changes do you need to make and what is the positive benefit of doing so?

(*List five changes you can make, and the benefits that each might bring*):

6 - GOALS

Why is it important to have goals? Well if you do not have goals you will not get anywhere. It is like getting on a bus and not knowing what your destination is. Yes you will travel and go places but what if they are places you do not want to be in. What if it brings you to a dead end? You could be going round and around for years. They say life is like a game of football: you cannot score if you can't see the goal post. You won't know where to aim. A goal is only a dream with a deadline. Goals are what drive you. It is what makes you get up out of bed in the morning. Imagine waking each day and not knowing what to do, where to go. It would be terrible having nothing to look forward to or to challenge you. By setting goals for yourself or your business you have something to work towards. Goals keep you on your feet. Often when we get down or find times hard it is hard to set goals you feel what is the point. Goals are things that you want to achieve. Places you want to go. Things you want to do. Some people are more "goal" focused than others but all individuals should have some goals and should set themselves targets for what they want to achieve. When you do not have goals you will often drift through life and get to eighty years of age and wonder how did I get here, what a waste, why did I not do all those things. Get focused now and set some goals. Small goals, big goals, wow goals. Get started before it is too late.

What kind of goals? Perhaps a holiday to Spain? A new car might be on the list. A big house in the countryside would be great. A million euros in the bank account would be nice. Learn a new language, whatever you like. Each section or part of your lifewheel should have clear and focused goals.

Under the following headings, list your goals:

- Health
- Finance
- Fun
- Relationships
- Community
- Personal Development

However you do not have to have goals in each section you may be happy in some areas so they can wait until such time as you need to set new goals. How do you set goals?

You write a statement for your specific goal. It must be stated in the positive and as if it is current.

For example: "I am the director of my own sales company and it is January 2016, and we have an annual turnover of €250K".

Goals need to meet the "SMART" criteria.

They need to be **Specific**, **Measureable**, **Achievable**, **Realistic** and **Time - based**. What does this mean?

If you say, for example, "I want to increase sales", that is not specific enough, it needs more detail. It does not say by how much. A more specific way of saying this might be, "I want to increase sales by

20%". That is more specific, but is it measurable? Yes, but it is a bit vague. You would need to be clear what figures your sales are currently at. For example; "I shall increase my current sales from €250,000 by 20% within a six-month period". This is more specific and more measurable.

Next, is it realistic? In most cases, it would be realistic but if your sales are diving due to problems, such as the recession, competition or other factors, it may not be realistic to attempt 20%, and your goal needs to be realistic. If you're aiming to join the RAF and you are colour blind, you cannot realistically become a pilot. Is your goal achievable? It may or may not be. You must look at it in detail and work out whether or not it is achievable. It may not seem achievable, but look at all your options. Who can help you and what resources do you have available to you. Remember! There were many times someone said that something could not be done and yet it was achieved. The four-minute mile was achieved by Roger Bannister. Soon after, this record was broken, others followed. So, often you can achieve the unachievable.

Next up is your goal time-based? What time frame do you have on your goal? Try to give it a realistic time. If it cannot be achieved in a certain time you can re-evaluate your goal and set a new deadline but do not keep pushing out the deadline or you may never achieve it. Goals need to be written down or you can forget about it happening. To increase the chance of you achieving your goals you should:

1. Tell someone about your goal. Someone who will support you and you're dreams. Someone who will push you forward, cheer you on. Hire someone who can encourage you, perhaps a personal coach.

2. Give your goal a deadline.

Write it down.

Refer to it often. Write it on vision board or in a goal book.

Visualise your goal. See yourself actually living the goal. How does it feel? What can you hear? What does it smell like? This is a very good tool.
When you set your goal you should break it down into action steps. What do you have to do to achieve this goal?

Task 13: Goal Setting. Write as follows.

Goal:

Deadline:

Reason for wanting to achieve this goal:

What will I gain from achieving this goal?

What will I lose and what are the risks?

Whenever you try to achieve a goal, something will suffer. If you go back to college, your spare time will be reduced and you might miss out on a social life. You may not see your friends or family so much. If you decide to give up your job to go back to college your finances will suffer. If you decide to train for a marathon you will not be eating rubbish and sitting watching the television. Instead you will have a training plan which will need to be adhered to and you will need to be fully committed to that training schedule. When your friends are all out having fun, you may be running those miles.

What will suffer? You need to look at your goals and weigh up what you will gain and what you will lose and you may decide that it is actually not worth all the effort.

List the resources available to you. Who can help you? What time do you have? What will it cost? Who can give you support. There is always someone who has done this before you and to seek the advice of a mentor or trainer or coach may speed up your progress and help you to avoid pit falls that you may not have foreseen. It is a good idea to work with a professional or a coach. Think of your "when, where and how."

Goals need to be focused on and you need to apply the 'Pareto' rule. This says that you should focus 80% of your time on your top 20 goals or priorities.

Why do people often fail to achieve their goals? They fail to start.

7. TIME MANAGEMENT

- Time management is the effective use of your time.
- Used correctly it will add value to your day allowing you to achieve more in less time.
- Reduces stress.
- Stress due to disorganisation – missing appointments, running late and so on.
- Stress due to over commitment to others.
- Stress due to poor planning and scheduling.
- Stress due to procrastination.

How much time do we actually have?

- 24 hours in one day. 168 hours in a week
- 1,440 minutes in the day
- 86, 400 seconds in your day

How much time are you wasting? How much time do you have left?

As I write this, I am 44 years old. If I live to 84, that gives me forty years, please God. If you work that out in months, I have 480 months ... not a lot is it? What do you want to be remembered for? We should all be aiming to leave the world a better place from when we found it. Live your life and do not die too young. Read this: "Here lies Clodagh Swanson RIP. Born

1967, buried 2015, died 2000". That means we may be here but we are actually dead inside. Find what is missing before it is too late.

Ask yourself the following questions:

Do you make action lists or to do lists?
Do you prioritise the activities or tasks you need to undertake?
Have you a cluttered desk or home?
Do you ever have difficulty finding documents, keys or papers?
Do you write goals for work and for your personal life and do you up-date them?
Do you finish all the items on your to-do list?
Have you a place to put everything?
Are you assertive?
Do you give yourself space to work quietly?
Can you relax when not at work, without thinking about work?
Do people know the best time to reach you?
Do you take steps every day to bring you closer to your goals?
If interrupted, does your concentration return quickly?
Do people who report to you work with enthusiasm when you delegate work to them?
Do you delegate well?
Are you often late for work or appointments?
Can you deal effectively with people who stay too long in person or on the phone?
Do you try to prevent problems before they arise or

deal with them in panic?

Do you meet deadlines with time to spare?

Are you under control or being controlled?

If you have answered honestly you may now go through each question and reflect on the current situation.

Do you make action lists or to do lists?

Each day you should have your day planned and it should cover all aspects of the day. Allocate time to your work. Allow plenty of time for sleep, fun and your family. You plan it from the time you rise to the time you go to bed. You make sure you allocate time for eating and exercise and allow yourself a 20% margin for interruptions and disturbances to your schedule. Each action should have the approximate time it will take you to undertake the task. See example of the time planner and ensure that each of your life roles get time to be fitted into the schedule.

One good tool to use is the box matrix which has four sections.

When planning your day and your week, and indeed your month, you need to be sure that you are working mainly from box II. This is the preparation and planning box. This is your proactive section your planning and getting ready well in advance of events and you are making sure that you have enough time for all you need to do, before it gets to panic mode, which is what most people end up working in. When you are not proactive and you spend your time on the wrong things or on unimportant things, you leave the important things to one side. Then what happens is you end up in a state of urgency and panic.

Another reason why people avoid doing the important things is that they may be procrastinating and putting off the jobs they do not like or the job may be too large. We shall talk about procrastination later but it is important that you actually do the job you do not like to do, or would rather not do, first. Always get the painful work out of the way first. This will allow you time then to enjoy the work you do like to do, also, you may experience the real "feel good" factor when you complete those horrid tasks and get them out of the way.

For me, I dislike doing accounts. I hate to have to do anything like that, so I delegate as much of that as possible. The stress of constantly being in Box I of the diagram is not a healthy place to be. You're under pressure all the time and your body can not take this long term. Some people become addicted to working under pressure in what some call urgency addiction, defined by the rush of adrenalin when you achieve those tasks with one minute to spare. You think you are great for getting it all done, for all the effort it took and the release when it was finished. But again, your physical body cannot do this long term. When your body is constantly under pressure, your adrenal glands will suffer and this can lead to many disorders and physical illness. They say that approximately 80% of illness now is due to stress. A notable point is that of the most successful companies in the world who achieve the most, they spend 65 to 80% of their time working in box II. The average company spends 15%. What does this tell you? They only spend 20 % of their time in box I.

Another method of prioritising is the ABCDE Rule:

- A= Crucial
- B = Important
- C = Little Value
- D = No value or delegate
- E = Eliminate

A = Very important it must be done or there will be consequences.
B = Tasks that should be done. Failure to do so will have minor consequences   but you may be able to live with that.
C = Something that would be nice to do.
D = Delegate
E = Eliminate, it makes no difference either way whether it is done or not.

Have you a cluttered desk or home? You need to work in an area that is neat, tidy and free from distractions. Where you are easily able to find items, files and folders easily and be able to find any documents that you need at hand. Clutter in your work area will result in clutter in your mind. It is a very good idea to put everything away correctly in the correct place when you are finished. This will insure that you are working in a clean and organised area and this allows you to be free to be creative, to find items quickly and to avoid the stress of misplaced items.

Misplaced items are so annoying! You're under pressure and suddenly you cannot find the stamps, the keys or the mobile phone. You have five minutes until the post office closes and it is panic, panic, panic. The best idea is to put everything in its own place. A key box or holder on the wall is a good idea, at home or in the office. One place for the phone, a stamp box etc. Keep your filing system in total order and ensure that all staff are familiar with where items are to be filed. They may all file in a different order.

Do you finish all the items on your to do list? Most times probably not. Why do you not get all the items on your list done? What happened to that great plan?

The phone rings eight times and you answer it. Every time your email in box keeps getting more and more full. Two people call to your desk and stop to talk. You go to get a coffee three or four times in the morning, never mind the afternoon. On top of that, you take too long for your lunch and before you know it time to go home with nothing done.

Well, what can you do about that? You will have to train yourself to become disciplined to ensure that people and things do not get in the way of your work. The phone can be put onto voice mail until such time as you wish to check it. For example, you could put a message on there to say I am unavailable until 1 pm at which point I will check messages and I will check my messages again at 5pm. This way people know when they can get you and when you will be checking. You do not have to answer each call or each text. If they really want to get you, they will eventually.

Emails again do not have to be answered immediately. The amount of time it takes to sort through them and then to reply it is madness. You do not need to answer each one. I hear you say, 'but they will be annoyed if I do not get back to them'. They will get over it. When sending emails you can add to it that you do not need the person to reply. This may avoid them sending in a reply which you do not need to see. Another option is to delegate and have someone else check them for you. This way any that require action can be given to you to do at your earliest convenience. Technology was intended to help us and to make our life easier, but I am afraid it has had the opposite effect for many.

Personally, I detest email as I get so many, most of which I do not need. A telephone call would be better! When on calls, do make sure you do not spend too much time waffling on and wasting time. Keep it short and end the conversation as quickly as possible. How can you get rid of a personal caller or a phone caller quickly? When the conversation starts, let them know that you have in fact approximately three minutes before you are due to take another call. Advise them that there call is important but you need to keep it to a minimum. If you need to, tell them you will call them back at a more convenient time. Advise them that you are in the middle of something or with someone and that you will get back to them. They may not like it but that is your time they are interrupting and time is money. Each time you say yes to that interruption you are saying yes to them and no to you. Whenever you take on someone else's workload your own does not get done. Learn to say no. If someone asks you to do something, tell them that you need to check your diary and you will get straight back to them. This will allow you ten minutes to actually think about whether or not you really want to do what they have asked. People will not like you for saying no, but they will eventually move on and get over it. They say "those that mind don't matter and those that matter don't mind". If you are in your office and you need to get something urgent completed, put a sign on the door and actually lock it. Again they will get used to it.

Can you and do you delegate? We are all able to delegate some of our tasks, be they at work or in the home. Most times though we choose not to. Why? We feel we need to do everything. To be the superwomen, or to be superman. "I will seem like a failure if I do not do this." "They will think I cannot cope."

These are all thoughts and assumptions in your own mind. Delegate and move on. There is no point having someone work for you if you are doing all the work. Believe me, I have been there. When a member of staff would ring me ask me to take over a problem, I did and this doubled my workload. Then I was reading Richard Branson's book *Screw It Lets Do It* and he mentioned the same thing. He said it dawned on him one day that he had hired the best people, so why was he not utilising them? So my new approach to people asking me to do their stuff was to pass it back to them. "Well I think you could deal with that. That is why I hired you. I hired you because you are bright, clever and can think on your feet. I think you can find the solution for yourself and let me know how you get on." Most times, they will deal effectively with the issue and it makes it easier for you to get on with your work. A manager manages. And a leader leads. Jack Walsh, when he worked for General Electric, would always try to hand back the issue or problem to the person who would present it to him and ask them what they think they should do with it. It also empowers people and eventually they should be coming to your door less and less. If you can google or research Jack Walsh's methods they are well worth a look.

How do you delegate effectively? Decide what tasks you would either not like to do or someone else could do better. Henry Ford, inventor of the Model T car, said, "I do not need to know everything or do everything myself as long as I know where I can find someone else who can." Delegate and free yourself up to do what you really want to do with your time.

What should you delegate and what should you not delegate?

You should delegate tasks that are routine. Tasks that can be done better by others, more qualified, more suitable and who have more time, skill or knowledge than you. Delegate the tasks that develop and empower team members. Delegate the tasks that will challenge. You can even do this with your children. Delegate tasks and empower them. If they do well, then they can have their allowance or their pocket money.

Do not delegate emergencies, tasks that require skill or tough decision making or tasks that require some form of monitoring.

There are some very good books published on Time Management. My favourite is by Stephen R. Covey, *The 7 Habits Of Highly Effective People*. He also has one called *First Things First*. Both are excellent books. Other favourites of mine include *The Four Hour Work Week* by Tim Ferris and also a book by fellow Irishman, Owen Fitzpatrick, called *Not Enough Hours*.

How to write to do lists:

First, create a general to do list.

Ask yourself, then "are there any items on the list that do not require action?"
Then:
Group the remaining items into a set of projects or tasks.
Put your life goals at the top of the list.
Review the projects and decide on which ones you want to progress with.

For each project, list the first, small actions that are required.
Create your delegation list and arrange to delegate those items.
From all of the above, prepare your next actions list. Remove all work that has been completed. Be sure to reward yourself even if you only write on them "achieved" and "well done".

At the end of each week, reflect on what you achieved and what you did not achieve. For those areas that you did not achieve ask yourself what stopped you? Are there any consistencies? Check and keep an eye on any patterns which emerge and do not serve you. Make your list for next week based on this and always aim to improve on the week just gone.

Leverage: How to use other people and other resources available to you.

In business, I am consistently amazed at the amount of time that top executives of companies waste. They are basically pouring money down the toilet. They will not hire a PA or a secretary. They try to do all tasks themselves and this ends up in them losing money big time in the long run. Or, they end up having wonderful staff and micromanaging them.

Task 14: Time

List five ways that you waste time:

List five ways in which you could change this:

8. STRESS MANAGEMENT

What is stress? Stress in your life is a physical and mental condition that could be said to affect everyone at some point, even children and teenagers. Stress is the feeling that you are unable to cope. Stress, the occasional time, is not going to do you any harm long term. We all have a little now and again. Stress over long periods of time will lead to general illness and much worse. Worry and anxiety over issues or problems will remain in your head quite often and when they stay there long term and are not dealt with, it can lead to chronic stress. Working under conditions which are not acceptable to you or where you are not happy in your work will result in you feeling resentful. You may dread going into work every day and the long term will wear you down.

Perhaps you are living in an abusive or loveless relationship. Not being accepted or respected can also be very stressful over a long time. Working too hard, long hours and not getting time out for you will all lead to stress. No exercise, no fun and no down time. The body is very similar to a car or a machine where in it will not be able to take abuse long term and needs regular maintenance to keep it in top shape. A person I know likened stress to a bag of stones. You have a ruck sack and you keep filling it with stones. Each of these stones represents a problem. The bag gets heavier and heavier and finally one more stone causes you and the rucksack to fall backwards. The straw that broke the camel's back! When you just cannot take any more.

What does stress look like in a person?

> Rushing around.
> Always seems to be in a panic.
> Short temper.
> May or may not become isolated.
> May be generally disagreeable.
> May not have any interest in general things.
> Always under pressure.
> May cry a lot.
> Often when someone is stressed they lose weight.

They often feel that each problem or situation is someone else's fault. They cannot actually see what they are doing to others as they are in a stressful state and often it is only when they come out of it that they are able to see how they had been acting in the previously.

Common causes of stress:

> Death
> Marriage
> Moving house
> Birth of baby
> New job
> Lost job
> Promotion

Reconciliation
Overwork
Christmas
Bored at work not feeling fulfilled
Holidays

That would not be the correct order. One by itself is not too bad you may be able to manage. But as with some people, they get married, move house and job at the same time and on top of all that someone dies. Well you can imagine the stress there and this actually does happen. Even the most wonderful things like a wedding or a new baby can cause mayhem to a life. Families fight like mad over wedding invitation lists. Is it all actually worth it? I laugh because actually one of the nice things like going on holidays can be such a stressful time, trying to keep kids in order on a four hour car drive to the airport, then long plane journey after having to repack luggage because it was too heavy and you do not want to pay extra for overweight. I've been there pulling stuff out of suitcases. Then all hungry, tired and cramped. To finish it off, the luggage gets lost. By the time you finally relax on holiday it is often the time to leave. A little planning and letting go will ease the stress.

Anyway all stressful situations can be reduced if you have a few techniques that we will mention later. But what actually does stress do to a body physically? Long term, stress can be incredibly harmful. It is now reported that 80% of illness is caused by stress. Ulcers, heart attacks, strokes, headache, backache. The list is endless! So let us look at briefly at what happens when our bodies are stressed:

Brain chemistry changes and it affects the production of serotonin, noradrenalin and dopamine.

Circulation is affected, heart is pounding and blood pressure is raised.
Hormones are affected such as adrenalin, prolactin, steroids and the thyroid gland is affected.

Immune system is weakened with changes in the white blood cell production and reduced resistance to colds and flu.

Digestive system is affected often with weight loss as a result of loss of appetite. Nausea, diarrhoea, and ulcers are all common occurrences as a result of stress.

Skin rashes, such as eczema and psoriasis and hair loss.

Psychological states such as anxiety, panic attacks and depression.

In summation there is hardly any system in the body that is not affected by stress.

Ways to reduce stress:

There are two points to consider. The first is the situation. The second is how you react to the situation.

The situation:
There may be nothing that you can do about the situation. What you can do is look at the way in which you react to the situation. You can react calmly and not panic, or react badly and let the situation run away with you, letting it take over completely. Often people just can't let things go. When you get upset, you are the only one who lets you get upset. When someone says, "he upset me", it is actually you that has allowed them to upset you. So you have a choice: to be upset or not, to be stressed or not. I say, when you feel annoyed or upset just get out of that space. You are the only one who can stress you or upset you.
   There is a lovely book called *The Four Agreements*, by Don Miguel. In this simple, book it has four guidelines for life:

> Be impeccable with your words. Don't hurt with words and do what you say you will do.

> Do not make assumptions. We often do this in stressful situations. We think that someone else is thinking something else. They are not generally. Do not make assumptions as you have no idea what someone else is thinking.

How often have you been under pressure and you're there thinking; "Oh my god, I will be late", "He will kill me", "I will be fired", and so on. All assumptions!

The third agreement is never to take things personally. I do this all the time and it is hard not to. However, if you actively try not to, it gets easier. I know now that often when someone is hurtful or unkind towards me it is because they are hurting themselves. When someone is very aggressive or badly behaved it is normally that they are hurting inside. What does it matter what someone else thinks?

Finally, the fourth agreement is always do your best. This is all you can actually do. In any given second and in any situation, we are all only able to do our best and if you know that you have really tried and could do no more, that should take a little of the stress out of the situation. We really are the creators of most of our own stress. Adding to our workload, taking on too much, not saying no to others. It is important to learn to say no.

Plenty of rest and good quality sleep:

Sleep is so vital to recharge the body. Some people need more than others. Maybe have a ten-minute nap in the day if you need to re-charge. Avoid caffeine from teatime, as well as any alcoholic drinks, as they will not allow a good night sleep. You may sleep and wake or you may not have a quality sleep, meaning it may be disturbed with on and off waking. Make sure you are warm. Personally I can never sleep if I am cold. Even camping on a cold night you can be warm enough. Milk is good to drink before bed as it has natural muscle relaxants and tryptophan, which helps to relax the body. Hot milk is perfect before bed or when you cannot sleep. Plenty of fresh air and exercise will also help to tire you out.

Relaxation or meditation prior to bed or breathing exercises will also help and have added benefits

Exercise:

A lot of people hate doing regular exercise but I am a person who was converted. I never did any exercise until I was 40. I never knew the benefits and I wish I had discovered it much earlier in life. When I began to run and could not get to the end of the road. "I will never do this", I thought, but week by week, I got better, fitter and stronger, to the point where if I did not get out for a run I would nearly go mad! Endorphins! It can be addictive, but hey, it's a good addiction. By exercising for at least thirty minutes a day, you are really helping to maintain that body. A healthy body and health mind should be side by side.

Exercise produces endorphins, "the happy chemicals", and they will make you feel better. I know you may feel half dead coming out of the gym but you will always be in a better mood than when you went in. Start slow and work up your fitness level. Start at a minimum of 30 minutes a day. Less is not enough.

Exercise will also get that metabolism going and help your body burn off fat and excess body weight. It will sharpen your focus with regard to your mental ability. I find if you get to the gym first thing in the morning at about 7am, you are set up for the day. It gets those happy endorphins going and you get the day off to a good start. Exercise will help to reduce stress levels.

Diet:

Diet is very important in a stress reduction plan. You are what you eat. Smoking, drinking and eating food which is not good for you is like putting rubbish petrol into an expensive car. It will clog up the system and nothing will work as it should. You want to eat food that is good for you. A balanced diet from the food triangle, with particular attention to the foods that make you feel good and are actually good for you. Vitamin c is said to be depleted when under stress same goes for the B Vitamins.

The B vitamins are responsible for a healthy nervous system which when we are under pressure often get depleted. B complex is a good supplement to take if you're under stress. Water is so important in any diet and most people do not drink it at all. Our body is composed of approximately 75% water so it is important to replace it daily. The brain cannot function without water and we need at least three litres a day. When we sweat, we lose water and we lose it at night too so it is very important to replace it and to stay hydrated. When you're under stress often you will find a person's skin becomes very dry. This is due to lack of water in the skin and the body and dry skin will show signs of ageing quicker than an oily skin. Not tea or coffee pure water. As you know you can live without food but you cannot live without water. When you are under stress, pay careful attention to your diet. People will often turn to comfort food, cigarettes and alcohol when under pressure and this will actually put more stress on the body. Alcohol is a depressant and may cause you to feel much worse. Alcohol may also cause panic attacks or affect the persons nerves making them feel a lot worse than before they took the drink. A regular detox would be no harm, but refer to a specialist as a detox may often make you feel terrible with headaches etc. Always speak to a specialist first.

Relaxation techniques:

People often find it hard to relax. If you're the kind of person who is going all the time you may find it very difficult to relax at all. There are some simple things you can do to help you relax.

Learn some relaxation techniques
Learn to breathe properly
Walk
Yoga
Tai Chi
Meditation

The list is endless.

One thing that runs throughout all of these things is the ability to empty the mind. To calm the mind and think of nothing. Again, this takes practice.

A simple relaxation technique:

Find a room that has no noise, soft light and no distractions.
Ensure that it is warm and comfortable.
Ensure that your clothing is not tight and begin.
Lie on the ground on your back and close your eyes.
Start at the toes. Be conscious of your toes. Feel them stretching. Tighten them and then release. Tight then relax.
Move up to the ankles and calf area next. Be conscious of your calf, and feel the ground under your calf. Tighten and relax.
Feel and be conscious of your knees.
Feel and be conscious of your upper thigh area. Tighten and relax.
Feel your bottom on the ground. Tighten and relax your buttocks.
Now feel your lower back.
Feel your abdomen breath in and out. Let the stomach rise and fall. Your stomach should expand when you breathe in and lower when you breathe out.
Move up the arms, starting with fingers. Clench the fingers and release.
Feel your lower arm. Tighten your arm muscles then relax.
Move up to the shoulders and raise and lower the shoulders.
Move to the face. Smile then relax.
Move up to the eyebrows and raise them then relax.

Each movement should be done three times, working your way up the body. By the end you should feel heavy and a little more relaxed.

Some of these movements can be done sitting or in the car, at any chance you get when you feel stressed or up tight.

Watch your posture. In general a lot of people keep all their tension in their shoulders and neck so if you are feeling, this rotate the shoulders a few times.

Massage and Aromatherapy:

Both massage and aromatherapy have been used for centuries to help clients relax. The romans indulged in this after eating and bathing. Massage has many benefits for the reduction in stress and for the general wellbeing of the person.

Benefits of massage include:

> Relaxation of tired or aching muscles.
> Lowering of blood pressure.
> Aids the elimination of waste from the body via the lymphatic system.
> Aids removal of lactic acid build-up in muscles and tissues.
> Improves general mobility of joints.

> When used in conjunction with aromatherapy oils, the benefits of massage work in synergy with the therapeutic properties of the oils. To help in the reduction of stress, there are many oils that can be used.

Chamomile can help you to relax and to sleep. It is good for a bath before bed time, or can be mixed into a massage rub. Chamomile tea is also beneficial for relaxing. Chamomile is very good for children too helping them to relax and sleep. It is anti-inflammatory also.

Lavender oil is excellent and one that is good for the first aid box. It is called the angel of healing. It is also good for baths and can be put on a pillow to aid sleep. This oil is also beneficial for children but it is not to be used in the first twelve weeks of pregnancy.

Marjoram is very good to help sleep and is like a sedative. You must check the contra-indications for this as care needs to be taken.

Clary sage essential oil will help you to fall asleep. It has a very strong effect and persons should not drink alcohol or take any other medication while using clary sage. It has a numbing effect and is also great for pain relief. The Native American Indians used to smoke this.

For depression related stress or fatigue, you can use some of the oils we call "the sunshine oils." They are used to lift your spirit.
Grapefruit, bergamot, orange, lemon and neroli are some examples of these. Neroli would be the best and very useful for depression. Geranium is ideal for

balancing the female hormones which often causes lack of sleep and stress just before menstruation. The male oil would be sandalwood. When adding oils to a bath, place a tiny drop of milk into the bath, with them as this will help disperse the oil. Water and oil do not mix. Before using an aromatherapy oil, please check for contra-indications that means check that it is safe to use. They can be very harmful if not used correctly. If using in a massage medium, you would mix 2 drops of oil to 5ml of massage medium. They are quite strong and are absorbed directly into the blood stream.

Visualisation techniques:

This is also a very good method for dealing with stressful situations or events. It is also very helpful in aiding you visualise yourself in any situation in the future. If something is stressing you, you can take some time to do some positive visualisations to calm yourself down and reduce stress. Some are for confidence, some are for goals and some are for stress reduction.

 Pick a place that you find totally relaxing in your mind. For me, it is the beach, in a hot country with the waves coming in. The sound of the sea, the heat of the sun, the feel of the sand between your toes and the sun warming your face. Think of this. Feel it, be there and relax. I always feel calm and relaxed in the sun. I love the smell of the sea and the sea weed. The breeze as it hits your face or the strength of the ocean. You yourself may have another picture. Imagine a peaceful beautiful green forest. Just go there anytime you feel you need to unwind or relax. A good visualisation technique to use when people are troubling you or stressing you is to see them with bunny ears or have them look like Mickey Mouse. They will not stress you as much, you will be laughing! How could you take them seriously? There are loads of visualisations on the internet and you will find tapes and CDs also on the subject. Remember when setting goals as discussed in the earlier chapter to use visualisation techniques. See yourself living the goal.

Some hobbies are very good for relaxation. Painting and art, pottery, swimming, reading, knitting whatever rocks your boat! So find a hobby that you can totally immerse yourself in and relax. If you do not enjoy the subject, you will not relax.

Acupuncture is a traditional Chinese treatment that I find very good for stress, illness and general health and wellbeing. I am never ill. Ever. I take care all year to take vitamin C and Echinacea, which helps to build the immune system. So I rarely get a cold which lasts longer than a day or two. However, if I feel I am getting bad, or have a lot of stress or indeed have no energy, acupuncture is my first point of call. When your body is stressed, often there is an imbalance. Acupuncture works on the meridians of the body. It is like a system of rail networks and if one rail line is blocked nothing can get in or out or function correctly. So by unblocking the area it allows a free flow of good energy or positive energy to the area. I will always immediately feel a little better and then great by the next day. Acupuncture is a very good treatment for stress relief; you can get lots of information on it on the internet or from a local practitioner. Remember; only you allow yourself to be stressed. Nobody can stress you. It is a situation. And as we mentioned earlier!

E+A=O

Event + Action (Response) = Outcome

Respond properly to stress and you will have a better outcome. Just walk away.

Task 15: Stress Reduction

List five things that make you stressed:

List one way you could reduce that stress in each case:

9. CONFIDENCE AND SELF - ESTEEM.

Confidence is a big thing. You're either confident or you are not. Can you work on your confidence? I would say yes. I think personally, your confidence has a lot to do with your upbringing and your conditioning. Conditioning means – to have a significant influence on or determine the manner or outcome of something. If you grow up in a home full of criticism or fear then there is a greater chance you will feel inadequate all your life. I know growing up in my home as a child, I was often very frightened. My father was often drunk and violent towards my mother and of course we saw this. We were always scared.

When he was not living with us we were always afraid of the next knock on the door. What if he smashed the glass? Constant fear will destroy your confidence. Later in my life if someone put me down, it also made me feel small and inadequate. I began to feel I was stupid and no good at certain things. I was told I was no good at finance. I loved finance in school. But I avoided the finance side of my business because I actually began to believe that I was no good at this. Actually, I was very good at it. I will explain later how to fix this.

Many grow up with abuse. It might be violent, mental or sexual, but it always leaves its mark. It shatters confidence. It can make a person feel unclean, dirty, or weak. It totally destroys the person unless they seek professional help and get support. It can be dealt with effectively. And the thing to remember if you are a sufferer of any kind of abuse is that you are a victim. Perhaps you were a wife who was verbally and emotionally abused for many years. You could be man who was bullied in the work force. Perhaps your wife left you. How could you have confidence after that? Perhaps your husband did not fight to save your marriage. Perhaps he let you walk away. Emotional abuse is far worse than violence some would say. As with violence, you can see the marks, often with emotional abuse you begin to doubt yourself. The bully often tells you that it is your fault. They actually tell you that it is you who is the bully. You are abusing them ... And you actually believe it. How the hell could you be confident with all that going on?

I grew up as a child in an often violent, fearful home and it most definitely had a knock on effect on my confidence. It was only when I was in my forties that I found myself, thankfully. Finally my time to shine!

I would not be the person I am today if it was not for them. I had loving aunts, uncles and cousins so I was lucky. A lot of people do not make it. My mum was busy working and had lost her husband in her thirties. Despite his issues, she loved that man. It was only later in life I realised how hard it must have been for her and how lonely. She got me through school and gave me some great gifts. I always value what I have and do not waste. I can make anything out of anything. And I work hard. As any girl knows when you split up with a boyfriend, it is heart breaking but to lose someone, especially to drown in tragic circumstances like he did, was a massive heartbreak for her. I did not have a great relationship with her at the time and it is only now I realise how much stress she must have been under. We used to hide from the rent man, or television lenience man the odd time. Most people do. It is funny now but then it was hard. I really appreciate my mum now.

Now here is a very important point. If you ask most people why they drink alcohol they say that it is to give them confidence. We need to find our confidence without alcohol. If you have been told as a child that you're stupid or have been ridiculed in school, which often happened then, how do you think your confidence will be? As a trainer, I hear stories all the time from adults who said that, when they were a child, a nun tied their left hand behind their back and they were told to write with their right hand. Or being told they were stupid because they had learning difficulties. We now know that people with learning difficulties are often smarter than others. Often they are smarter and more creative than the so-called smart people. We have Richard Branson, Whoopi Goldberg, Tom Cruise to name three well-known figures all with dyslexia! How do you think your confidence would be if you were told often enough you were stupid? If you were told you are not bright? Look at Thomas Edison he was told he was stupid; and he invented the lightbulb. If you are told you are ugly you may believe it.

Anyway what am I getting at? What we are told and the way we are treated will result in who we are. The good news is it is always possible to become more confident. There are many ways.

If it is something that has been said to you or the way you have been treated you may need help on your journey with this. Emotional support and counselling is a positive choice for severe confidence due to abuse or bullying, you most definitely need to get help. Over time, this will get better and you can recover fully to become the beautiful man or women you truly are!

Task 16: Confidence

Let's have a look at ourselves:

- Are you afraid to say something in case someone laughs at you?
- Do you feel guilty if you have to say no?
- You do not allow yourself to make mistakes? In other words, "you beat yourself up?
- Do you feel you have to agree with others?
- Often have negative thoughts about yourself?
- Often do not feel as good as others?
- When deciding to do things you would like to do you feel guilty?
- Do you feel guilty spending on yourself? You are afraid to have fun?
- Are you afraid to try new things with new people?
- Are you afraid to talk to strangers?
- Are you afraid to strike up a conversation?
- Do you walk with your head and shoulders down?

If this is you, my guess is you are not all too confident.

A confident person will:

- Strike up conversations and not be afraid.
- Will try new things without worry or too much fear.
- They will set goals.

- They will measure and achieve their success.
- Often they have a care-free attitude.
- They will walk tall shoulders back and they will smile.
- Often they look younger as they frown less. No worry lines.

In order to be confident, you need to get rid of self-doubt and you need to stop all that negative self-talk and get rid of those negative limiting beliefs.

When I did my career-coaching course, my tutor told us about the monkey trap. It is a very good analogy. When they try to catch monkeys, they cut a hole in a tree and place rice or food in there. The monkey then puts in their hand and grabs the food, in their fist. Then they cannot get the hand out. My tutor then asked, how do you think the monkey could get free? "What do they need to do to get out?" What do you think you need to let go of to be free? What do you need to let go of to be more confident? In this story, all the monkey had to do was actually let go of the food and then they would be free. What do you have to let go of? (Thanks Eoin.) Monkeys would often die a horrible death instead of just letting go. You can have a horrible life too if you do not learn to let go.

You looked at your limiting beliefs in chapter 3, but it would be no harm to review that list again now.

Task 17: The Good List

Now let us make a list of all the good things about you. Not so many? Well, that needs to change!

Look at all the negative points, and really look at them. Did anyone actually tell you that you were no good? Did anyone actually tell you that you suck?

And if they did, decide right now that what they say does not matter anymore. You do not believe it anymore and you do not care anymore.

Let us now change all those negatives feelings about ourselves to a more positive feeling. Let us try to rephrase the limiting beliefs.

Negative: I am a bad mother.
Positive: I am the best mother I can be at any given time.
Negative: I suck at everything I do.
Positive: I can only try my best and I am not perfect.
Negative: She will never go out with me.
Positive: I have a 50% chance that she will.

You get the idea. Turn all your negatives into *Positives:*

Re-write your list now.

List five of your negative beliefs:

List each of those beliefs turned into positives:

The main way to develop confidence is to learn to like yourself.

Take the following steps each day:

- Eat well
- Sleep well
- Exercise
- Avoid negative people
- Treat yourself to something nice
- Spend some time in nature.
- Do your gratitude list, remember the attitude of gratitude.

10. ASSERTIVENESS

Assertiveness is not aggressive behaviour. It is having the confidence to do and say what needs to be said and done. It is not pushy. It is respectful and allows you to maintain the individual's dignity.

Task 18: Lack of assertiveness

- Think of a time when you needed to be assertive and you were not.
- How did you feel physically in your body?
- Where did you feel it?
- Close your eyes and think back to that time.
- How do you feel now thinking of that event?
- What do you wish you had done differently?
- The next time this happens I will react as follows:

Task 19: Assertive Person

Think of an assertive person you know. What are the characteristics they display?

List these top five characteristics:

You might have listed:-

- Calm, speak with a low voice
- They are challenging in a nice way.
- They appear confident.
- They walk with their head high and shoulders back.
- They maintain eye contact.

To be assertive, you need to feel secure in yourself. You need to be able to say what needs to be said. Assertiveness comes from you feeling strong enough to make a comment or express a view without worry of what others think. It is about you feeling happy with yourself. Think about this: A person consistently asks you to do something, for example, to mind their child and it is always you they ask. You do not say anything, because you worry about "what will they think of me", or "if I say no it will cause a row". You need to stop thinking about what they think of you. Instead think of the feeling you get and the sense of resentment this creates each time this happens when you are asked to do something you do not like to do.

Learning to say no! This is a habit like any other. The first few times you say no to someone you may feel a little uncomfortable. But slowly, it will become easier.

If someone asks you to do something, tell them you need to check your diary and you will get back to them, or tell them that you would really like to help but you have your own items that need to be done first. Ask them if it is possible to ask someone else. For example, I was a people pleaser I used to be a yes person. What does this lead to? Well essentially it takes the monkey of their back and places it on yours. When you keep doing something for someone else that you do not want to do, it makes you resentful, even angry. Anger is a dangerous sometimes unhealthy emotion. It may lead to illness and it is not good to hold it in the body. "Holding onto anger is like drinking poison and expecting the other person to die." (Buddha).

There is a story of two monks who are walking alongside a stream. They find a fair maiden who needs to get across. The older monk carries her to the other side and the younger monk after much time and much resentment says to the older monk. Why did you carry her so far? The old monk replies I left her at the river bank it is you who is carrying her. The resentment was in the young monk. We do this all the time. Anyway back to assertiveness.

Review times when you were not assertive – list them. And then list the ways in which you would do things differently the next time.

Task 20: Reactions

Example:

Incident: Mary asked me to have her children again this weekend and I could not say no.

My reaction: I could not say no. I felt so angry and it kept niggling me all day and into the next week.

What would or could I do differently next time: I should have said to Mary I need to check I think I have something on. And actually do not give an answer there and then. Get back to her when I check my own schedule.

11. BUILDING RELATIONSHIPS

We all have relationships, unless we live on an island alone. We have relationships with our parents, partnership relationships at work, husband and wife, child and parent. Teacher and student, employer and employee; the list is endless! Why is it that some people more popular and have better relationships? Why do some people attract a lot of people to them? They people magnets? Why do people feel better after being with them? They are skilled at building solid relationships. This is not an easy thing to do. It does come easy to some people while it is more difficult for others. You may be shy, but that should not stop you from having, strong and loving relationships. I think a few things are very important.

Be yourself. When you try to be something or somebody else, it can be very false and people see through it. Maybe not at first, but eventually they will. Always tell the truth. If people find you lie or tell white lies, they will not be able to trust you. Nobody likes a liar. I have often had people lie to me about serious things and when I realised I was never ever able to trust them again. It is worse when it is someone you love. You know, some people have no problem telling lies. Be truthful and, as the little book *The Four Agreements*, says, "be impeccable with your word". Do what you say you will do and keep your word. Again, letting people down is really bad for relationship building. People will say you are unreliable not an attractive characteristic. The best relationships are built on trust.

At work, if you say you will do something and you do it people know that you can be relied upon. If you are late or do not attend to what you say you will do your relationships will suffer. They will not be as strong. People like positive people. They want to be around them ... Unless they are a miserable person and then they will just want to be with miserable people! I do not like to be around negative people I find they drain me. Physically! So I do not let them into my space. If they do enter I do not stay too long. I think you attract a mirror of yourself. I believe that you get back what you give out. With relationships, people want to be with someone who is fun to be around.
One of the key skills for relationship building, I have found, is the ability to listen. I think I am a good listener but I have actually had to work on this skill.

When I did my coach training, the importance of listening was of paramount importance. Coaching is all about listening. When we coach we spend most of our time listening. I have found while teaching adults for twenty years, that often when there is a problem in any respect, all people want is to be listened to. Quite often once they are heard, they park the problem and no more is said about it. We all think we are good listeners but very few are.

When you listen you should be clearly looking into the person's face and making eye contact. I know that when there is trouble in a marriage or relationship and you feel like you are saying the same thing for years. It is so draining and frustrating as you think "why the hell are they not getting the message?" or "Why are they not listening?" Perhaps they just do not care enough to listen because if they cared they would listen. Perhaps they will listen when the relationship is over.

How to listen

There are different types of listening:

- **Pseudo listening**. This is where you actually pretend to listen but really you have no interest what so ever in the fact that the cat had eight kittens or the bus was full.
- **Appreciative listening**. This is when we actually appreciate the topic it is of interest to us. We want to listen.
- **Empathetic listening**. This is normally when something bad happens or the person is telling you something sad, you listen with compassion and you normally attempt to be empathic or sympathetic in order to connect emotionally.
- **Comprehensive listening**. This is something we really want to listen to, like your favourite rock star, actor etc. You use comprehensive listening when you are following instructions or directions.

Nearly every aspect of life is improved by effective listening, including our organisations, corporations, schools and the everyday workplace.

Here are some barriers to effective listening:

- Interrupting someone: Thinking you know the answer and butting in. This is actually rude. Basically interrupting the other person is effectively saying that you do not value what they are saying, and only what you have to say is important. It may be worth trying this. Count to three after the person has stopped talking before you start. Effective listening means you listen, you do not talk.
- Trying to help or solve the problem in your head means that you are not actually listening. If you give the person your undivided attention, it is the purest act of love you can give.
- Treating a conversation as a competition. This is one of the worst things you can do. Trying to respond to a comment with a comment about something you're better than the other person etc.

It is also amazing how we understand and comprehend information. We pick something up and it is totally not what the person actually meant. So clarify if you are not sure, do not make assumptions. Giving constructive feedback to the person is also a good strategy. They then know that you have listened properly to them.

Other problems with listening occur when someone else will not stop talking. When you have good listening skills, you are likely to be more successful. We are given one mouth and two ears for a reason. So we can listen more than we talk. Talking more than is necessary is a barrier to effective communication and effective listening.

- Think before you speak.
- Practice self-control.
- Do not interrupt.
- Avoid useless talk for the sake of it.
- Keep it brief.
- Watch the other person's response or their body language.

The receiving stage: You are receiving information. This involves hearing and attending.
The understanding stage: The listener determines the context and meanings of the conversation.
The evaluating stage: In this stage, we critically assess what has been said. We evaluate it. What impact does this have on us? The thing to remember here is that our past experiences can affect how we accept information. If you have someone give you advice or try to help, you may take it as being bossy or controlling and that may not be what was actually intended. We coaches call this our blind spots. When something that has been said irritates me, I think, "What is that brining up for me?"

Often, it is not the person talking it is something that was said or done in the past. By developing awareness in your own body and feeling what is going on you may be able to deal with this before there is a rash or impulsive reaction.

Again, thinking before you speak. When people upset us, we allow them. You have a choice not to react or not to respond. Often saying nothing is the best response.

"When you talk, you are only repeating what you know, but when you listen, you learn something new." (The Dalai Lama)

Basic surface listening: All parties are talking and not really listening.

Attentive listening: The person listening is actually listening. Perhaps because they want to, where by there may be something in it for them. Alternatively, they may genuinely be interested in what the other person has to say. There is more to this though. You are also listening to non-verbal communication: Body language. What are they saying with their facial expressions? What are they not telling you? Often when I am coaching a client and they tell me "all is fine", I can tell from their eyes that all is not fine. The eyes show sadness and a depth. I see it. You need to be conscious and willing to truly be present to tune into that. When you are telling someone something, I am sure you feel hurt when you know they are not listening to you. You say, "you are not listening to me." Often you are talking and they are, for example typing, or then they take a call in the middle of a conversation. Not only are they not listening, it is rude. Try for one day to totally listen. Focus on what people are directly saying and listen. Listen with your eyes and ears. You will be amazed how much better all your relationships will be. Just try it.

Relationship building is more than just listening, even though listening is vital. Relationships need a few other ingredients.

With all relationships, they need time to develop and grow. Trust is a vital component and that takes time. Whether it is a personal or a business relationship trust is essential. Patrick Lencioni says in his book "Five Dysfunctions of a Team" when building a team the first pillar of the teams foundation is trust, if you do not have trust you have nothing. BNI the business network say that you do business with people you know like and trust.

How do you get people to like you? You firstly just be yourself. Try and find common ground or common interests. A great book that deals with this topic is *How To Win Friends And Influence People*, By Dale Carnegie. It is a brilliant book, and one of the most commonly praised books for business and life success. In this book, Dale mentions the importance of remembering people's names, for example. He says always to make a point to call someone by their name. Personally I think there are a few other small things you can do.

Random acts of kindness:

Do something for someone else. It is even better if you do without them knowing. Let someone go ahead in the line. Let someone out before you. Buy someone a bunch of flowers if you know they are having a bad day. I always remember a priest at mass saying one day. "Give someone flowers while they can enjoy them." What he meant was not to wait to give flowers when they are dead. Write a letter to someone who may be alone. I have a habit of sending people cards for everything. If someone is kind or does a favour for me, I send them a note to say thank you. If someone is doing a good job, I send them a note to say thank you. Most people just want a little recognition and appreciation. When someone does something good or nice let them know you appreciate it. Most bosses never tell their employees or their team that they are doing a good job. Never! How sad. Most employees leave their job because of a person, a manager or boss. Not because of money. Would you like to be the best boss in the world? That does not mean you're a softy or a push over. You could be fair, and you could get a great job done, but working with a team that are loyal and that like you and support you. You can do that all by building relationships.

Tips for building a positive relationship:

Create a safe environment where people are not afraid. And always apologise quickly when you know you are wrong. Always forgive. Forgive the person, perhaps, not the actions. Remember when someone does something wrong or bad, it is the behaviour that should be discussed as wrong or bad, not the person that is bad.

In times of conflict, try to separate the facts from the feelings. Has something in the past left scars and it is being brought up now and this persons approach to you? Perhaps you need to look at this. Is it your baggage or actually what they are actually saying? Often it is best to walk away and deal with the issue later when you have had time to think and to calm down. Do not react. When someone is hurting you realise that they may be in pain and that is why they are hitting out. Try to understand. They say that anger is frustrated love. There is nothing worse than frustrated love. When you love someone deeply and you cannot get your message through to them, it can get very frustrating and what is worse is when they do not actually even care. Have compassion for the other person at home or at work. You can have compassion and empathy and still be a good boss, even a tough boss, but a boss that has compassion and empathy when required. In most relationships, the problem is that we do not make time for the relationship. We are always too busy. Too busy to say, "I love you, I care about you, you're a great kid, you're are a terrific mum or dad. You're a brilliant teacher". We wait until it is too late. When the other person is gone!

Can a dad have a relationship with his kids if he works 24/7? Or a mum who is too busy to read a story or colour a picture. When we say no to those requests we are actually saying we do not care about spending time with you. Washing the dishes sometimes seems more important than reading or playing with your child, I have done it myself, but now I try to be with the person properly if I can, especially my children. Another important point in a relationship work or home is lateness. When you are late for someone else it says I do not value your time. It is not good to be late when building relationships or otherwise.

When there are times when you cannot get your message across then perhaps you could write down how you are feeling. The other person has to read it and it may help both of you. When a relationship breaks down there are many things you can do to try to fix it. However sometimes things cannot be fixed. Perhaps one person want to fix and the other just stays the same. You can live in that relationship and be unhappy or you can leave. You can be happy alone. An empty relationship is worse than none at all. Relationships take two people to build and to maintain. Do not take for granted and feed the relationship with love and appreciation. Say what you need to say before it is too late.

At work build powerful relationships through respect and trust. Be appreciative and give people recognition bring them with you. Be compassionate and work with empathy and kindness in the workplace. This will develop and nurture key relationships and people will go above and beyond what their job descriptions state. They will be on your side and they will build your organisation. If you want to judge your success, judge your relationships. In organisations worldwide they talk about managing people, they need to lead people to set an example and to build relationships.

Building relationships – Recap Tips:

- Become interested in other people. What makes them tick?
- Always wear a smile, and use the person's name.
- Make the other person feel important and listen… really listen?
- Spend time on the relationship.
- Do not act negatively, be positive and give appreciation and recognition at every single opportunity.
- Always look for the good. Count your blessings.

Task 21: Building Relationships

What are the most important relationships in my life? How can I make these even better?

(List five examples)

What is not working?

(List five examples)

What external relationships need improvement or care?

How can I bring all my relationships to the next level?

12. Dealing with Conflict

Conflict is a natural occurrence. It is often very productive in the workforce and should be viewed as a positive intervention for idea generation and moving forward.

However when conflict becomes troublesome or painful, it needs to be addressed. What does the word conflict mean? By definition:

"Come into collision or disagreement; be contradictory, at variance, or in opposition; clash" We have all been there!

When people interact, live and work together it is normal for disputes or misunderstandings to occur. People have different values and beliefs. They may come from different backgrounds, countries, races or religions. Of course there will be disputes. Often there are not too many differences but when people get stressed or under pressure they fall into a conflict situation as they are perhaps, tired, over worked, emotional and not feeling their normal self. As we said earlier, when people are under pressure consistently their immune system and their health suffers and often they are not able to deal with even the smallest of problems. Often a comment or situation that they could normally deal with, they react badly to, maybe shouting, becoming angry or even abusive and violent. They are not behaving normally. Other individuals are just always in a confrontational place. They have to disagree with everything. They are negative and never have a good thing to say. They may be in need of a coach perhaps. We have all met them.

Your home or your workplace needs an environment that people can thrive in. If there is conflict, it is very upsetting. Long term it can have divesting effects. House often in turbulence still haunts me now. As a child you feel afraid, unsafe, you feel worried. When is it going to kick off again? I always remember a counsellor telling me the worst thing ever for kids is to be in an environment like that. Conflict and shouting. Do not do it in front of your children. It will stay with them forever. Everyone in the environment is affected by the conflict, not just those involved in the actual conflict. It is no different in the workforce. This environment is often no different to a family situation. At work you also need to feel safe and secure. Everyone at work is affected by the conflict, not just those in the heat of it.

Dealing with personal conflict:

The golden rule is to deal with it. It will not just go away. Often it goes away for a while, but it is like plastering over cracks in a wall. Eventually it comes back and often worse.

Deal with it immediately. Even if it means saying "time out", "take ten and we will talk about this in ten minutes".

If it is a home or personal relationship try to stop talking and actually listen yourself. This is really hard. You want to be heard. But if you let the other person let off steam perhaps then you may get a chance to be heard. Sometimes they just need to rant. I remember with one of my sons he would come in and suddenly everything was wrong, the kitchen was wrong, the milk was wrong, the tea was wrong, and I just knew that something had upset him and actually it was not me. In time, I learned to leave him and not push him, keep out of his way until he calmed down. That could have been the next day. A hug might have helped. At 16 he was six foot tall, but he still needed the odd hug. I needed hugs from him too. Boys also have a lot of internalised conflict. Their body is changing, their becoming adults and they do not know how to verbalise their emotions. The least thing can cause them to become angry. That anger needs to be expressed. At home often the conflict you find in relationships is due to conditioning and the way in which the individuals have been brought up. You know we are all doing our best at any one time and we may not have the tools to do any better at the time. However there are many people and tools out there now that you can access for help.

Sometimes you just need to say "I am here if you need to talk". Reassure them and try to talk at a later time when you know they are in better space. Sometimes a person will avoid talking about something that needs to be discussed. Avoidance of conflict can cause massive problems. Left, the issue just festers and grows bigger and bigger.

There is also a kind of passive aggressive conflict which is subtle. This leaves the person receiving it feeling like they are going crazy. They do not even realise that is happening. It is a form of abuse and bullying and would fall under conflict. Smart comments and insults by one person to make the other person feel small. The person giving out the insult is often in a bad place and is hurting themselves. However this does not mean that you should excuse the behaviour. When it is consistent or habitual then you may need to confront the behaviour and tell the other person that:

A. They are doing it. Perhaps they do not know that what they are doing is actually hurting you or disturbing for you.
B. It is not acceptable.
C. Ask them what their reasons are for doing it. Why?
D. What will they do in future? Will they change?

If they are not going to change then perhaps you should not be in that relationship. It will crush your confidence and take away your self-esteem. When you hear negative things said often enough you may begin to believe them. If you are told that everything is your fault, you will eventually begin to believe it. Often the bully will tell you that in fact you are the bully. You are not. You may need professional help.

If you are experiencing this, confront the person and tell them that this is not acceptable. Challenge them. If they say something, challenge them to explain themselves. To be honest, in most cases, you are wasting your time and you may need to decide that it is better for you to just move on. Protect yourself and move on. People live like this for years, walking on eggshells, afraid to say anything! Soon, they stop communicating.

Conflict in the work place is common.

When and where? The team meeting is a perfect setting. Everyone is trying to be heard. Often racing ahead in the conversation and trying to outdo each other. Or they have to be the one to talk. This is the usual one person who says everything, another one who says nothing and one who throws the eyes up to heaven. Meetings need to be run effectively. One good way to achieve this is to have something to pass around. The person holding the object, a tennis ball, for example, is the only one allowed to speak and no one else is allowed to speak until they are finished. Everyone gets a turn to speak and offer their input. No interruptions! There is a great method using the book by Edward de Bono, *Six Thinking Hats*". This 'six thinking hats' method is great because it cuts down meeting times dramatically and actually gets great results fast. Another good method is called "time to think", by Nancy Kline.

At work you have people who consistently cause drama by blaming others for their poor performance. If anything goes wrong they claim it is not their fault. They shift the blame, they tell lies. They insult others. Hide the truth and so on. There are often tears, drama and what is worse is when the person responsible for the team, the manager or the leadership team may not do anything about it. They hope the problem will go away but it will not. In this case, this needs to be dealt with swiftly. A true leader or a good manager will not accept this nonsense. All people involved will be held accountable.

What causes conflict at work? Jealousy, competition, under performance, cheating, gossip; the list is endless.

Two things are always involved in conflict and often both together. Communication and emotion! With communication, often we are not told something or you are told something at the wrong time. You hear you are not getting promoted from the person, who did get promoted, this should not happen. Information is often not being communicated in the proper fashion by the right person. This is a massive problem in industry. I remember a family member getting news that their jobs were being lost on the national news station instead of hearing it from the organisation that they worked for.

Communication of information needs to be clean, clear and concise, delivered at the right time, in the right medium.

The other big factor is emotion. At work people need to keep their emotions in check. They need to take the emotion out of the situation. In order to think logically and not react with emotions. Now sometimes a little emotion is required but it is learning and knowing when to react with the right measure and type of emotion that is important.

So how do we deal with conflict in the workforce?

Well, it starts with defining what is acceptable and what is not in terms of behaviour. What are your values as an organisation? I always refer to ours if there is a dispute. Are we for example behaving in a respectful manner? If not, we are actually breaking our core values with is certainly not acceptable. Are they breaking a code of conduct? Things like job descriptions are also very important for when something goes wrong. Are they behaving as they should?

A very clear line of command is also necessary often. But if everyone understands their role and the organisations values and what is acceptable, it should be easier. Look at the situation and try to get a win/win for your outcome. Aim to keep everyone happy. If it is win/lose, well then someone wins and someone else will lose. That is not ideal. Compromise is important here. The person who is willing to compromise will go a long way. A true leader does not have to be seen to win every battle.

Is this conflict actually worth worrying about? What is really important?

Reflect on this.

In his book on the "five dysfunctions of a team" Patrick Lencioni states that fear of conflict is one of the dysfunctions of a team. You need a certain amount of conflict, however; it is vital that the conflict be managed and facilitated in a healthy and safe environment. It is highly productive, innovative and creative. The next time, think is it worth it? Is this productive?

Often the best thing to do is to take ten minutes and come back calm and try for the win/win. Use empathy to review the other side of the situation. Empathy is one of the greatest gifts you can have. Use it wisely.

Whenever I am in a confrontational situation I always ask myself how is the other person feeling? If I was in their shoes how would I feel?

Task 22: Conflict

What areas of my life are confrontational?

When in work:

When at home:

How do I feel about this?

What is it doing to me as a person?

What do I really need to do to address this?

13. EMOTIONAL INTELLIGENCE

"It is with the heart that one sees rightly, what is invisible to the eye." Antonne De Saint- Exupry.

Emotional intelligence became very popular as a result of Danial Goleman's work. Did you know that more and more scientists believe Emotional Intelligence (EQ), not IQ, is the most important factor in determining a person's success? Well I personally agree.

Quite often you see a very clever person and they cannot communicate with others. They are not able to deal with the real world. They are not as popular as some of our emotionally intelligent people. Whilst we are told in the work place to leave our emotions at home, there is more and more scientific research showing the importance of the emotional link to the brain. The brain is very complex organ and there are two very important brain sections we use when we interact in the world.

Emotional Intelligence refers to the ability to perceive, control and evaluate emotions. Some say Emotional Intelligence can be learned and strengthened. While others claim it is an inborn characteristic.

Original research was conducted by Peter Salovey and John D Mayer. They say that "emotional intelligence is a subset of social intelligence that involves the ability to monitor one's own and others feelings and emotions, to discriminate among them and to use this information to guide our thinking and actions.

Four Branches of EQ:

- Perceiving emotions: To understand emotions you must first accurately perceive them. Including non - verbal language and body signals.
- Reasoning with emotions: Using emotions to promote thinking awareness and cognitive activity. Emotions help prioritize what we pay attention to and react to.
- Understanding emotions: Carrying a wide variety of meanings. How do de we interpret emotions?
- Managing emotions: Effectively managing our emotions.
- Research now claims that EQ is more valuable than IQ
- They say that only 20 % IQ = Success in life.

Data now shows that children are more troubled emotionally than before. They are lonely, depressed, angry, unruly, more nervous and prone to worry. They are more impulsive and aggressive. We need to learn to deal healthily with our emotions.

The nervous system:

- The brain is the control system for the body.
- When we have an event, the brain takes in the event and processes it, through sight, touch, smell, and so on.
- It is processed in two ways: logically and emotionally.
- Which happens first? Research now shows it registers emotionally first.
- We have two minds: The logical mind and the emotional mind.
- It is the emotional mind that captures the upper hand, swamping the rational mind.
- Limbic system – complex set of brain structures near the cortex concerned with our basic emotions. Long-term memory, motivation and behaviour.
- Amygdala – Small almond shaped structure in the temporal lobe of the brain that controls our emotions.
- When our brain senses something, it has two sets of wiring: one goes to the logic centre, while the other to the emotional centre.
- The message gets to the Amygdala quicker through a back door. Hence, we often react before we have time to think.

Emotional intelligence consists of self-awareness. That means being aware of self. Self-regulation is then the management of self. Motivation is our internal or external drive to achieve goals. Empathy deals with how we manage our relationships. Social skill is how we influence responses in others. As you can see these are very important skills or traits to have, and, as with any skillset, they can be improved at any time if you desire to do so. They certainly need to be on every high-flyers list.

Self-Awareness:

This means, in short, firstly being aware of our mood, and, secondly, how we feel about that mood. Knowing ones internal states, resources, preferences and intuition. How do your emotions affect others? Knowing your strengths, your weakness or your limits. Knowing what you can do. Self- confidence: What are you worth?

"Anger is never without a reason, but seldom a good one." – Ben Franklin

Self-awareness is vital to success in today's world. Knowing when you have said the wrong thing. Or knowing when your emotions are running riot. Knowing when you are stressed. This self- awareness needs to be developed and worked on. We have blind spots. We can only see so much of ourselves. We need to start to listen to our body. We also need to understand how we feel about how we feel? Why do we react this way or that way? Why does that person push my buttons? Why do I always react so badly to that person? When we are coaching we ask you those questions. When something annoys you, you need to ask yourself, "Why is it bringing up those feelings?" And remember:

E+R=O (Event + Response = Outcome)

How you respond to something will dictate your outcome. Bad response = bad outcome.

The hallmarks of self-awareness is confidence. How can you become more self-aware? Start listening to yourself. To your head talk and to your body. What is it telling you? Where do you feel it in your body?

Self-regulation is the ability to think before acting. Manage our reactions and to keep disruptive emotions in check.

Trust is maintaining honesty and integrity. Your word is your bond. What you say you will do. This is often hard. But you can learn to do this! Practice and count to ten. I know I am a very emotional person and often I feel very emotional about something. I need to go take time out to actually reflect. In the past, I would jump in and have my say and fight my corner, but we can often say something we regret. This is vitally important in the workplace. Do not rashly react. Stay calm and think. Self- regulation is about the ability to redirect our moods and our reactions.

Conscientiousness is about responsibility. This trait is lacking in most individuals. - They have a "blame" mentality and it is always someone else's fault.

Conscientiousness is one of the greatest traits a leader could have. The leader takes the blame. The buck stops with me. It is highly commendable and unfortunately in short supply.

Adaptability which is, again, very much lacking. You see this all the time. "Well we have always done it this way we cannot change." Adaptability is vital to business success or indeed life. If something is not working, are you going to stay there and just let it get worse? Or are you going to make changes? Adaptability is vital for business success. Reaching new markets is all about being adaptable. It is as, they say not always the strongest that survive, it is the ones willing to change course! Adaptability is essential especially when things are not going to plan. This is not to say you run from things when they are not working you must first try to make them work. Try to find solutions. If, finally, the best thing to do is to change course, then change course. Adapt and change and often you will be the winner, leaving those behind who were not willing to change.

Motivation. People with high levels of emotional intelligence tend to be very motivated individuals. They are not always motivated by money; generally they are intrinsically motivated by other inputs, like making a difference, being useful, finding a reason to get involved. People with high levels of emotional intelligence tend to be very active and dedicated to what they decide to put their minds too. They are driven and often passionate about something. They keep going even when times are hard and challenges present themselves. They have a "never give up" attitude. They make things happen and one of their key attributes is optimism. They persist. They have a drive to achieve. They set goals, big goals and they go for them. They are committed and they follow through. They finish the project and they see it through. They show a massive amount of initiative and are always ready when opportunities arise. They create opportunities where there were previously were none.

Empathy. The ability to put yourself in someone else shoes. To completely be able to feel what they are feeling. To be able totally understand. Empathy is not sympathy. In customer service and working with the public it is about anticipating, recognizing and meeting customer's needs. I think this is the greatest emotional intelligence trait. It is so vital for life. No matter what you are doing, whether at work or in the home, when you are communicating or dealing with others it is vital to be able to listen and to actually ask yourself "well, how would I feel if I was them?" Perhaps you have to give someone bad news. Or someone has to be let go at work. When dealing with this, the ability to place yourself in their shoes is vital. Think, "How would I feel if I was told my work was not up to standard?" How would I feel if it was me being told this.

Social skill. Daniel Goleman defines this as:
"adeptness at inducing desirable responses in others.
He discusses the ability to influence. How to
Persuade? The art of communication and the vital
one, being able to listen. Being able to deal with
conflict effectively and so that everyone wins.
Leadership! Inspiring others both individuals and
groups. Acting as a change catalyst and developing
and building strong bonds. Adapting collaboration
and cooperation and building strong teams.
   Social skills are an essential part of our behaviour.
This is really important. We are social animals by
nature. We are not meant to be alone. Social skill is
vital in everything you do. It is your ability to get on
with others. To be a likeable character! Social skills
are the skills we use to communicate and interact
with. This is done through our language, both verbal
and non-verbal. Also through our body language and
through how we dress and how we present ourselves.
Social skills are the key to developing and building
friendships and building strong bonds with others.
When you are trying to do things in life we can always
achieve much more if we do it with others. If we work
as a team and pull together! Can you imagine a
project team of artists, designing a piece of publishing
or a construction company trying to build a house?
One man alone could properly do it all but it would
take longer, take more effort, physically and mentally.
Not only would the person need all the skills, they
would also need all the knowledge. It would take
longer and would ultimately be lonely. It would be far

more fun working as part of an inclusive social group. However there would be the usual drama of people trying to get along with each other. However, great things can be achieved when we pull together. Social skills some people just do not have. They are not able to connect with others. They do not know how to have a proper conversation. Social skills are about connections. How do you build those skills and what are they. It is not always those employees who are the brightest who will bring in the most revenue. Quite often it is the sales representative that is liked and trusted by the customers. He firstly listens to what they want. Then he arranges to give it to them. When organizing teams, companies and organisations would be well advised to choose EQ over IQ. BNI, a business networking organization says, "People buy from people they know, like, and trust." How do you get to know people? Simple. You listen, you have conversations and you build bonds. You have empathy and you feel what they feel. Just like them. Or at least you try to find common ground. You have a sense of humor and you develop a like for that person.

Trust, well that again takes time. The best way to build trust is to do what you say you will do. Be there on time. And do it on time. Always try to under promise and over deliver. No phonies! People see right through it, maybe not at first but eventually they will. It takes a lifetime to build your reputation and a second to destroy it. In business, they say the top competencies are empathy, influence and initiative.

Steps to working on those social skills:

- Avoid the shyness. Try to come out of your shell.
- Try to get involved in conversations. Speak to people that would normally be out of your comfort zone.
- Build your confidence and self- esteem. Like yourself. No one else will like you if you do not like yourself. Smile. It is the prettiest thing you can wear.
- Be around positive people and get involved.
- Be kind to others. Try to do a good deed.
- Develop a strong sense of humour. Remember when people feel good around you it produces the chemical hormone oxytocin which makes us all feel good. Those chemicals, when produced often enough, with the right people, build life-long bonds, which, in some case, can travel the globe.

Daniel Goleman in an article on 'leadership that gets results', talks about these as the key strengths a leader needs to bring to the table.

Task 23: EQ Trait Development

What emotional intelligence traits do I excel at?

What are my weak spots?

Am I aware of my traits? What would others say if I asked them?

At work, what emotional intelligence traits should I sharpen and what ones should I address?

14. INSPIRATION & MOTIVATION

To lead your best life you must be inspired and motivated otherwise you will just have a life. To achieve great things and to live life to the max, you must be motivated to do so. What motivates us? Well, we are all different and what motivates one person may or may not motivate another. Does money drive you? Or is it recognition? Do you want fame? What motivates you?

The word 'inspiration' may mean any of the following:

- A feeling of enthusiasm and encouragement you get from someone or something, which gives you new ideas or the desire to create something.
- Arousal of the mind to special unusual activity or creativity.
- A product of your creative thinking and work.
- A sudden intuition as part of solving a problem
- Arousing to a particular emotion or action.

And what does the word motivate mean?

- To give an incentive for action.
- Provide someone with a reason for doing something.

- To make someone feel determined to do something or enthusiastic about doing it.

We all have different reasons for doing things. What I want you to do now would be to become inspired and motivated to have a wonderful life. What would inspire you or motivate you to action? Well, many things could. I remember someone told me how a friend stopped smoking. He tried so many times and failed. However once his young daughter came to him and started to cry. He asked her why was she crying and she said, "Well, you are going to die". "Why do you say that", he said. "Because the man on the television said that smoking kills you." He never smoked again. The instant realization of his daughter's worry and love for him was enough. Often in life, we are never inspired to change or motivated to change until the pain gets too much. However when something is waiting to blossom and when the time is right and the inspiration or motivation is high enough change can take place. You see this often in life when the husband trades the wife in for younger model. So the wife starts to go to the gym. Perhaps has a makeover and so on. We find an old photo of ourselves looking slim, tanned and beautiful and we say to ourselves what have I become? The shock often inspires us to action. Often though, inspiration or motivation comes from a more serious event. Perhaps someone experiences a heart attack. You go through a sudden death in the family or death of a friend. It hits you between the eyes and you say. "That is it. I have had enough I must change before it is too late."

Perhaps you neighbour gets a new car. It motivates you to work a bit harder and longer in the office, get the bonus and hey presto! You have your own new car.

But why am I writing about motivation and inspiration? Well, often we are inspired or motivated by the wrong things, so it is important to know what and why you are motivated. A boss needs you to work late and says: I will pay you an extra 100 euro! That does not motivate you. But if he says you can have an extra day off next week to spend with your children, now that might motivate you. Other times motivation is about our intrinsic values. I am a fair person and justice is very important to me being a Libra. If something is very unfair, I am motivated to do something about it. I do not like poverty and hardship and to be honest in the western world we know very little about true poverty. If you go to India or Cape Town to the Shanti towns, then you will see poverty. I am motivated by things that I am passionate about. It is all about passion. What makes you come alive? What would you die for or fight for? Me? I am passionate about education and the right for each child to have food, an education and a loving supporting environment. My children are passionate about animals and hence two are vegetarian so what motivates you?

Looking back over my life I guess a lot of what I was trying to achieve was for recognition. I remember never feeling good enough and the teachers did not help. If you're told you're going to fail, my attitude is "prove them wrong." I am the most stubborn person I know. This can be good but it is also a character defect, of which I have many. However if you channel that stubbornness, it can be great. I got qualification after qualification and someone, said "what are you trying to prove?"

I guess what motivated me was achievement. Setting goals for myself and reaching them. I do not think I did that to impress anyone. I did it to challenge myself and to prove to myself. Poverty is a great motivator. Most times, we sit back and we are happy to get buy just doing what we do. Often only when hard times come along and then we are motivated to act. Try new avenues to get work. Do the extra few hours, to go the extra mile. Growing up, it is amazing how many people from working class backgrounds did really well. They had to. They had to educate themselves and get out of the poverty trap. I always said to students, "Girls, this education will take you from social welfare and poverty to earning more than accountants." A clever beauty therapist can earn over a thousand euro a week. And many have become multi-millionaires! All you need is passion and a desire to succeed. However, hard work always plays a massive part. People do not see the 16 or 18 hour days and the no weekends off. Success does not fall into your lap. Work for it. It is amazing that most millionaires are self-made.

WOW! You see, everything is possible. I really believe that. Back to motivation!

I watched a television program once about a man who was a builder and he went to South Africa to the shanty towns. In a week, he had built 5, perhaps 10, houses. I cried and I was inspired to do the same. I thought, "I really want to do this." Many years later after trying year after year to get a place, I travelled to Cape Town with two thousand builders (yes, two thousand builders!) and in one week we built 250 houses. It was amazing and it inspired me to do more. We saw the difference we could make to the lives of people the other side of the world.

What motivates me now and inspires me? Working with people and organisations and helping them to find their own path, or more often, a new path. I absolutely love when someone really is lost and does not know what to do or where to go. When we work together not, only do they often find a new direction they find a new life. They find their confidence and their self-esteem soars. The magic happens. They say things like, "My whole life has changed." That is priceless.

I once had a group who sent me a card to say thanks for believing in us. That motivates me. Seeing a man, down on his luck with no ambition, fulfil his dream of becoming a nurse, going back to nursing college and following his dream. That inspires me and motivates me. And of course, my wonderful children who coach me and make the world a better place just by being in it.

Nature and the abundance of nature is just awesome and I get so inspired by it. There is always the calm after the storm. The calm of the forest, the abundance of the earth itself! The roar and strength of the ocean. Life is inspiring. But the people in it are often negative and do not see this. Help them to open their eyes or move on. As Helen Keller said, "The only thing worse than being blind is having sight but no vision".

I started to look at what motivated famous people. Richard Branson said he was partly motivated by a wish to prove himself when he started his school magazine. Later in life, he was motivated by people in the music industry. He said they were motivated by their convictions and selling records. They were passionate. He said he was never short of motivation, just cash.

Anthony Robbins, one of my favourite coaches, who I was lucky enough to see, said that one day he just had enough. He had bills and an eviction notice on his door and that was the last straw. He decided to change his life. The pain had obviously gotten too much.

Shakespeare wrote his sonnets after a broken heart, as did Billy Joel. Don't you just love where the inspiration sometimes comes from?

We are all inspired and motivated by different things. For Mother Teresa it was the pain and suffering of others. Lady Diana wanted to eradicate land mines. People tend to be motivated by what makes them tick internally and about things that are close to their hearts. You can often find out what motivates you by looking at your values. What is important in your life? Your life today is a reflection of who you are and the choices you made. However, it is never too late to make new ones. Be an inspiration to others. Two teachers in my daughter school were an inspiration to the students. Mr Walsh and Mr Burke! Well done! You are leaving the world a better place and as she said, "the teacher is a legend." What more could you ask for!

Task 24: What motivates and inspires you?

What are your passions?
(List five:)

What inspires me every day?
(List five:)

What makes me get excited?
(List five:)

What motivates me at work? When you know, tell your boss! It is only when you know what truly motivates you will you move forward at a faster pace.

How can you increase your motivation? Well, let's say you are setting goals:

On your vision board, you could list out the benefits of getting that goal. If you want to lose weight you could put a picture of a lovely dress on the vision board and visualize yourself in that dress, or the same for the new car.

If you need to get a promotion, list or affirm in your head how much better your life will be when you get there. Remember you will meet road blocks and you will have set backs, but that is ok. You start again and you just keep going. Often failure motivates us. Look at Abraham Lincoln: He lost how many elections at first often it is the failure alone that motivates us!

15. Happy at Work

"Do a job you love and you will never work day again in your life."

Why did I choose to talk about this? Most of us spend so much of our time in our jobs. At least 35 to 40 hours a week. 80% of people are said to be unhappy in their jobs, so I am writing about it because it is extremely important. When I was in secondary school, we had two problems. Teachers, whose approach to students was ineffective. Many were snobs. We also had career guidance teachers who were useless in that role. This is still common today. The role of a career guidance tutor is so important.

You were either going to college or you went working. If you were not going to college, the school really did not care about you. The career guidance teacher in most schools were useless and possibly dangerous in some cases. Do this or do that. The amount of people who want off to do careers they hated was crazy. People doing 8 years of medicine to please mommy or daddy! This is also common. As I said before, Johnny wanted to be an actor not a doctor. What a recipe for disaster.

Also the choice subjects were very narrow. The choices now are really no better but what is far better is the range of courses: Beauty, sports science, fashion, radio production, film production and the list is endless. Our youth have much more choice now.

Potentially, they have a better survival chance as hopefully they can find a course that suits their needs and their passions. There is also much more emphasis on returning to adult education and those who did not have a chance earlier could do an access course and get into college that way. As I write this, The College of Surgeons in Dublin is publishing a study of students who got in through the traditional methods and those that got into college through the back door. The result was that both faired basically the same. I could have told you that. When you are in school you do not know what you want half the time. Secondly, the educational system in second level school consists mainly of subject you may have totally no interest in. However when you go to college and it is the course of your dreams, you could be top of the class.

Why?

Firstly, you are interested and, secondly, you are motivated. It was so funny all the professions like trades that in the past they said were for dim people who could not go to college. I see beauty salon owners and hair salons having made millions. My son does DJ work and Calvin Harris made over $40 million last time I checked. So basically, what the hell does anyone know if you are passionate about what you do? I say you can easily earn a living.

Do what you love and if you do not know what you love, keep searching until you find it. If you look hard enough it will find you. You know when you are there because you will be excited. You will be passionate and your being will tell the world that this is what you were born to do. Your eyes will sparkle. It does not matter what your job or role is in life as long as it makes you happy. It is all about passion and what makes you come alive.

I remember a story about a man working in the space station and he was a cleaner. When asked what he was doing his reply was that he was helping put men on the moon and he was. Part of his role was to support the full organization. A hospital porter who wheeled people into theatre day in day out was asked why he had not gone home, when it was way past his finishing time. "Just one more he would say." They said "Why do you do that? Your back is broken, old and in pain." "Well he said I am saving lives."

We make a difference to the world, no matter what our job title is.

People say, "But come on, I have bills to pay! I cannot follow my dream job." Well I am telling you, basically, you can. You can do whatever you want whenever you want. Do not let anyone stop you. It may take years to get there but believe me you will do it.

But what do you actually want to do?

I always ask adults these questions.

- What makes you excited?
- What are you passionate about?
- What are your hobbies?
- What would you die for?
- What do you believe in?
- What are your values?

What did you want to be when you were a kid?

And do you know what the saddest thing of all is? They have no idea. They have completely lost themselves to society and its demands. Society rules us to conform. We have lost our inner compass and our identity. May you find yourself now, before it's too late!

If you do not know what you want, do you at least know what you do not want? That is a good place to start. Make a list of all the things in a job you would not like and would not want to do, such as:

- Indoors or outdoors?
- With a team or without a team?
- Shifts or day hours?
- Travel or no travel. You get the idea?

Here are quite a few Career Coaching tools! Try them. You may be amazed at what comes to mind.

Task 25: Career Wheel

Look at all the sections of the wheel and identify on a scale of 1-10 how satisfied you are with that section (one being really not satisfied and ten totally satisfied).

Any that score less than five need attention. Make a list of those that are low, and then make an action list of what you can do to make that better.

Score the following from one to ten:

Career:
Working relationships:
Rewards and recognition:
Motivation:
Security:
Personal development:
Passion and purpose:

Anything scoring less than five needs to be addressed.

Task 26: My perfect job

What would my perfect job look like?

Where would I be?

What would I be doing?

How much would I be paid?

Task 27: Time Line

If I had one year to live and I had to work, what would I do and where would I be?

If money was no problem, what job would I be doing?

What one regret to I have about my career?

What do other people say I would be good at?

Task 28: Strengths and Weakness

Make a list of your strengths and weaknesses. And please ensure you are kind to yourself! We all have strengths. Don't focus on the weakness. Remember this is related to work/career only.

List five strengths:

List five weaknesses:

Task 29: Work Place Skills Analysis

Indicate how you rate yourself, as good or weak, in the following areas:

- Organisation
- Planning
- Listening
- Writing
- Communication
- Interpersonal skills
- Financial ability
- Artistic ability
- Creativity
- Teamwork
- Time management
- Problem solving
- IT skills
- Teaching
- Management
- Leadership
- Conflict resolution
- Negotiation
- Delegation
- Musical ability

Task 30: Trait Analysis

For each of the following traits, list which ones are 'you' or 'not you':

- Honest
- Reliable
- Sincere
- Loyal
- Sympathetic
- Empathic
- Friendly
- Supportive
- Kind
- Appreciative
- Approachable
- Adaptable
- Flexible
- Affectionate
- Considerate
- Direct
- Perfectionist
- Doubtful
- Optimistic
- Pessimistic
- Modest
- Focused
- Determined
- StubbornPersistent

- Adaptable
- Flexible
- Affectionate
- Considerate
- Punctual
- Accountable
- Confident
- Realistic
- Conscientious
- Dependable
- Disciplined
- Independent
- Critical
- Judgmental

Task 31: Skills and Traits

What skills and traits do I need to improve moving forward to help me in my work and life?

List the five skills or traits that you think would be most useful to you now:

Well that was a lot of self-analysis. Should you wish to do this with a professional all the career coaches out there would be delighted to help you. You can look on the ICF (International Coaching Federation) Website for a list of coaches.
WWW.Internationalcoachingfederation.org

There are other tools that are really useful when looking for a job or a change. There is a selection of what we call "psychometric profiling" or testing assessments. I like the "Jung Type" Indicator myself and also the emotional intelligence trait testers. This one is free and it is really a very good one. Check out www.humanmetrics. It does personality assessment based on Extravert traits or introvert traits. It also goes deeper then into Judging, Feeling and Perceiving and intuitive. So you may get a result like this.

INFJ – so that means Introvert, Intuitive, Feeling and Judging. Check out the website for more details.

There are also other good assessment tools available such as the "Myers Briggs" test, which is probably the best known. There are many more, including a really good one called DISC. There are leadership assessment tools and sales tools to help select people who are suitable in those areas.

However, these personality assessments are not always 100% accurate, as people often give the answer they feel is wanted. The other point to consider is the frame of mind you are in when you undertake the test. Are you relaxed and have you enough time to do the test at your leisure?

There are emotional intelligence assessments and I love these personally. They show your EQ skills as opposed to your IQ. I love the EQ subject. There are also Value based indicators and they are good when you are looking to see what motivates a person.

Have a look online or contact the professionals. On average, you would expect to pay €150 per test. Companies would be wise to undertake these tests if looking for a key member of staff, like senior and middle management and executives. A wrong hire could result in a loss of time and money for any organization. A psychometric test, interview and culture fit are all good ideas prior to being hired.

So you now have an idea of your perfect job. How are you going to find it?

Most jobs are not advertised so how will you get the job of your dreams?

If I am working with a job search candidate, we take the following steps. We answer the following questions.

Task 32: Put it all together – what do I want?

Consider the following in your ideal job:

- Job Title:
- What Industry?
- Location?
- Salary?
- Potential companies to contact?
- Who can help me
- Do I need more training?
- First Steps?
- Is my CV up to date and adequate?
  (Have this professionally looked at by an expert.)

- Most people who type your CV or say they will do this for free are not very good.
- Is my cover letter really good?
- Deadline:
- Research the companies:
- Get the job!

As mentioned above, most CV producers are terrible. You really need someone who can sit with you and write a really good profile. Most organisations will not read past the profile. If it is not professional, dynamic and is lacking the "wow" factor, forget it. The CV also needs to be a maximum of two pages, no more. With a professional career coach, like me, we will work through it and tear it to bits until it is perfect. We will say in ten words what most say in a paragraph. It's all about impact. IMPACT! They do not want to be bored to death with long details. Keep it to the point. Short and direct.

Two very important points. In your CV you must remember companies are only interested in two things:

1   How you can make them money.
2   How you can save them money.

With every statement you make about yourself, you should ask what the impact of that was? What was the result for the organization?

Do not make the mistake that most people do, which is sending the same CV out to 300 companies. That will never work and you might wonder why you do not get an interview. Each CV needs to be tailored for the specific job to which you are replying. I hear you say, "I could not be bothered doing all that." Well do you want the job or don't you? Finding a job is a full-time job! You put a few hours into it each day if you're job hunting. Some companies in Ireland have up to two thousand applicants for a typical administration role. So you need to ensure your application is noticed.

As I mentioned, your profile is vital. Here is an example – one I used for a coach/trainer job and, importantly, it is all true:

Highly skilled, knowledgeable coach and educator, with a passion for bringing out the best in individuals. Excellent communication and interpersonal skills. A highly organised planner. Proven leader and motivator. Dedicated and driven. Enjoys working through challenges. Proven business ability. Passionate about and actively involved in the coaching and educational industry. 20 years teaching experience at third level. Cost aware and customer focused. Excellent levels of emotional agility.

Your letter must be attractive enough for them to want to meet you.

You must ensure that your CV and cover letter contain the words that they have used in the job specification. Yes, it is hard work but it will be all worth it if you land that top job.

Most people I meet for career coaching really cannot praise themselves enough or at all. This will get you nowhere. Your CV must be a marketing tool for you. I remember a girl calling to my office with a CV for a teaching role. The document was in a poor quality plastic folder, with grammar and typing mistakes on the CV and the print was slanted up the page. I thought, "she did not even bother to reprint this." To me that said poor quality and a "could not be bothered" attitude. She did not get an interview, never mind a job. Ant the terrible thing was that we were actually hiring. Part of her role would have been to produce notes for her students. Was that the standard she would provide? Well, I rest my case. I remember there was an organization I really wanted to work with. I thought I would never get in. The "I am not good enough" again. My limiting beliefs! But the "want to do" so was far too great to stop me so I said, "Give it a shot anyway." I stuck the organisation's logo on my vision board as you do and I prepared a nice letter, CV and copied all my diplomas and certificates. I purchased a lovely leather folder and organised the contents and off it went. I said "they will laugh at me." No. I got work. And I am still getting work.

Now along with the CV, you do need other skills. People skills! Know how to influence and have conversations. There are two great books for this, one I mentioned earlier: *How to Win Friends and Influence People*, by Dale Carnegie, is an old favourite, and the second is called *Influence* by Robert Caldini. Try to read these then put the contents into action in all you do in life. Believe me. I got an interview and the rest is history.

The other thing is that once you get the job, you have to keep it. You might be capable but if you're not likeable and good with people they will not keep you for long. Another time, I mentioned to a fellow coach that I was looking for work. He told me about an organization that may be hiring. Straight away the lovely leather folder and my secret contents went off again. And yes, again I got work. In some cases, this meant an extra €800 or €900 a month. It pays to get active. Ask for what you want and then make it happen. Often we are told about opportunities and we do nothing. No action, no results.

As a self-employed person, I am looking for a job each day of my life. I am sending out information on my company. I am writing tenders and submitting the same. I am talking to people and I am networking. Each day as a self-employed person I am looking for work. It is not going to come up and say, "Hi I am here". You have to go find it.

So let's now say that you have identified the organization or organisations you wish to work for. Next you must write the CV. And the most amazing letter! There are two types of letter: one is a letter of application for a job that has been advertised and the other is a letter of enquiry, which would be for a job that has not been advertised.

There are two main types of CV. You will need to decide which is best for you. I feel, and it has been proven right with my candidates, that the functional CV works best for most roles.

Always put yourself in the position of the reader. They do not want to be bored to death. They do not have time. So be direct to the point and use impact. And remember, it is all about results and what you can do for that organisation. I always hire for personality over skills. Skills can be learned and developed. Once an asshole, always an asshole! (Excuse the usage of this.)

But really a person's greatest asset is their personality. A smile goes a long way. Simple things like a positive mental attitude are also always admirable. I would take a personality over a PhD any day.

What is the best method to get a job? Well the numbers change all the time. But as a rule: Here are the worst:

- Looking for employer's listings on the internet: approximately at max a 10% success rate.
- Sending out curriculum vitae to companies directly: 7-10 % chance.
- Local newspaper advertisements: at a max 24% success rate.
- Employment agencies: 20-30% max.

The best ways:

- Knocking on doors with a smile: up to 50% effective.
- Going through phone listings and contacting companies directly approximately: 50% effective.
- Networking, using contacts that you have family, friends and old contacts: approximately 80% effective.

And the most effective of all is when you decide to follow your heart and go for the role or the vocation that is made for you. It always works. Approximately 88 to 95%.

But remember be realistic. Our physical abilities may limit us. But always, always go for what you really want in life and settle for nothing less.

So now that you have found the job of your dreams, what is it at work that makes you happy? We are presuming this is a paid employed role where you work for someone else.

I would say the most important thing is the culture of the organization. Is it like a family? Do people feel safe? Is there trust? Do people feel that what they do makes a difference? There is nothing worse for me than to do a job if, even though it paid really well, I felt I was not being appreciated. Or if I feel dead walking away. Organisations where employees feel like family work well and achieve massive results. Companies need to stop with the fear and start with the trust. Locking cabinets and timing tea breaks. Having a Hitler supervisor watch your every move. I read a really good book by Simon Sinek, called *Leaders Eat Last* and it talks about this. It is well worth a read. Could you work with someone who did not trust you? Fear is not productive. A happy, secure and well treated member of staff will be far more productive because they will want to contribute and they will want the company to achieve because they are that company. It amazes me to see CEOs and leaders fail on this all the time.

Happy at work means working with others. Being part of a team. We all think we know what a team is. But do you really? A team is not just a group of people. A class is a group of people but a team is a collection of people with a common goal and a common commitment to results. If you do not have this you are not part of a team. People wonder why teams do not work. There is no commitment. There is often commitment to themselves. You see this in sport, when each football player is trying to score the goals for the glory. That is not a high performance team, it is about the self. The high performance team will put the needs of team members above the self. Read some books on teams, particularly *The Five Dysfunctions of a Team* (Patrick Lencioni). It is a brilliant book and can be read in one night.

You will know you're happy at work when you wake up ready for action. There is no sigh and there is no heavy feeling weighing you down. You feel you can change the world. You also feel the time fly and, before you know it, you're heading home. So often I hear people say, "I cannot leave my job, I have bills to pay". Bullshit. Make it work. Leave the job and find a job you love before it is too late. Your family want a happy mum or dad. Stop making excuses. Come home each day with a smile and be happy. When the family ask, "How was your day?" you can say "Amazing!" I can say that when I am coaching or doing my mentoring clinics. I am really blessed. But I had to do that. I had to leave the safety nets, burn my boats and say, "I am not going to give up. I will make this happen." Approximately 20% of coaches make a living out of our profession. Most give up and go back to industry. I don't give up and neither will you. That is the easy way.

As Robert Frost said, "Two roads diverged in a wood, and I, I took the one less traveled by, And that has made all the difference".

"Travel where others fear to tread for this road shall deliver your treasures." (Clodagh Swanson)

16. LEADERSHIP

A leader is a person who rules, guides, inspires or commands others. Why have I chosen to talk about leadership? Well, to me (and to help you shine) I think leadership is very important. Leadership qualities for example are found lacking far too often. We do not develop these skills, we do not seek them in our children and we do not praise people and organisations often enough for being or producing leaders. High-quality authentic leaders are very hard to find and their development can start as a very young child.

Why do we need leaders? Without leaders there would be chaos. Everyone doing their own thing. No rules or regulations, people without direction. Could you imagine it? Leaders play a vital role in our lives. There are what we call good leaders and bad leaders. And to be honest a leader is a leader – good or bad! Who decides? Many would say Hitler was a bad leader. But let us not get confused with the behaviour. He may have been a bad person, we all have our own feelings on that one, however as far as leadership goes, he was a highly effective leader. Why? Because of the followers he had. Rightly or wrongly, he had millions of followers. Look what was done under his guidance. Mass murder and death on a truly horrific scale. I went to Auschwitz some years ago and it was horrid to witness what was left of the concentration camps. This man was a leader, but his actions were horrific.

On the other end of the scale, we have Mother Teresa. A true leader, and a small quiet women who changed the world. She was one of the kindest leaders ever to have walked the earth, and spent her life helping others. Imagine that at 18 she left India and travelled to Ireland to join the Loreto Convent in Rathfarnham, Ireland. Later, in India, she left her convent and began to work in the slums with no supplies, no equipment and no funds. She was to change the world as they would know it. A true leader. For me what leadership is about is this: doing the right thing. Even when all those around you think you are crazy, when people say you are mad, when the world is against you and people laugh and put you down, a leader will do it all against the odds. Quite often they are criticised and laughed at. They may even have to die for what they believe in. But a leader stands up for what is right. They have an inner compass that directs them and when things go wrong as they will often do they change direction, adapt and keep going.

Some great leaders of our current day include the business gurus Steve Jobs and Sir Richard Branson, Oprah Winfrey, Barack Obama, Lady Diana. We could go on and on.

I think that as humans and parents, we should always be aiming to be a better leader. Or to even just be a leader. Why is it that some people will not stand up and say what needs to be said, or do what needs to be done? Are they afraid of being criticised? I think so. Leaders do this naturally. Often they are scared, but they will go there anyway. Leadership is a lonely place, I always say. I wanted to talk about leadership so that, as part of your new life, you will become a better person. For me that means being a leader. Leaders have certain qualities and traits. Some people ask are leaders born or made? Certainly you can work on your leadership style and your leadership approach. However personally, I feel that true leaders have an innate ability to lead. They are different from a very early age. Perhaps their early life conditioned them? Who knows!

What personality traits do leaders have and what traits should they have:

- **Courage**. For me this is vital. The courage to say what needs to be said. To stand up for what is right even if the world is against you. Martin Luther King comes to mind. Knowing that you could die for your beliefs and convictions. As he did. Courage to stand up for others. Courage to do the right thing. To take a chance or a risk when you may fail. It is better to try than to regret not trying.

- **Compassion**. I believe that leaders have compassion. They can feel the pain of others and they have a great sense of empathy. Not always. I am talking about positive leaders not leaders who can do harm by their actions. We saw great compassion in the life of Mother Teresa and Lady Diana for example. Their actions were those of love and compassion for others. True servant leaders.

- **Vision**. They can see what others cannot see. They look to the future and dream big. They are dreamers often. They can view things with a long-term perspective. Their vision is so big that nobody believes it is achievable. Martin Luther King had a dream that little black and white children would one day play together. I visited the human rights museum in Atlanta and it was amazing. He was a great man. He paid the price.

- **Honesty and integrity**. They do what they say. They are accountable and they will always deliver on their promises. They will not let you down. Their value systems and beliefs are what they live by. They are accountable.

- **Kindness**. They are kind. They are willing to help others without wanting something back in return. They will support others and help others achieve their dreams. They will be givers not takers. Often they take no glory for their achievements. They say 'we' not 'I'.

- **Servants**. Leaders are often servants. They will serve others. They will do so without wanting praise or recognition for their efforts. Often no one will even know they are the leader. For anyone who wants to succeed in business they should read the leadership books by Robert

Greenleaf.

- **Commitment**. Leaders always commit to things. They will commit to do what they say they will do. They will be a vital part of any team as they will always follow through. They will also get others to commit. They will motivate and help others to achieve.

- **Competence**. Leaders must be able to "do". Be able to have abilities in certain areas. They must be competent at delegation, organization and communication. What they are not competent at, they will pass to someone who is. They will ask, who can do this job better than me. A typically weak leader will struggle, will try to do everything and will not be willing to pass it on. They think that passing it on is a sign of weakness. It is actually a sign of strength. Henry Ford said he did not need to know everything, all he needed was to know who knew. It also means having a proven track record in what you do. There is a very good quote on this point: "Managers do things right, leaders do the right thing". (Peter Drucker)

- **Character**. What does that mean? It is the full set of attributes that one has. Work ethic, humility, compassion, integrity, honesty and reliability. The way in which we conduct ourselves. People buy us before they buy our products. It is about trust and likeability. They are honourable.

- **Fearless**. Leaders need to be able to face fear and move forward. Most leaders may be afraid to do something or to try something. But they will. Because the pain of not doing it is much worse than the pain of doing it. They say pain is temporary, but the pain of not doing it stays with you forever. You're in pain anyway, so you may as well get a result from it. Whenever I feel pain or I find things difficult to endure I say to myself, "pain is temporary, pain is temporary". And the pain goes away.

- **Communicators**. Leaders must be able to communicate and get their message across, to be able to get people on board. The way you communicate is vital. You can gain or lose followers by the way you communicate. They say listening is the most important part of communication. Most people just want to be heard. We have two ears and one mouth for a good reason. Speak less, hear more. What makes a good communicator? They listen. They maintain eye contact, they have an open body language. They would obviously have empathy in bucket loads. They are genuinely interested in others and want to know all about the people they interact with. They will use effective body language. They will not beat about the bush, and will be direct when they need to be. Again, straightforwardness is a valuable leadership skill. Leaders in our community or workforce need to have a range of leadership styles. You cannot always be nice and you cannot always be an autocratic dictator. A good leader will know when to use what style. Their leadership styles are like golf clubs in a golf bag. Each has a different purpose. Knowing which one to use, and when, is vital.

What kinds of leadership styles are there?

The most obvious? The authoritative leader. The boss. They tell everyone what to do and you do not question it. His way or no way. That is fine and you may need to do this sometimes. If the building is on fire, you need someone who will act instantly, to direct and issue directions about what actions should be taken. It is not the time to sit down and say, "Let's collaborate here. What is the best way to evacuate the building? Let's have a team discussion here". No, at this stage the leader just says, "Let's get the hell out of here". At other times the leader may use a coaching or a collaborative style which encourages input and participation by the members of the group. This is good for individuals as they feel part of the decision-making process. What they think actually counts. Often the leader will make the final decision, however, he will have had input from those around him. The main leadership styles are:

- Authoritive
- Collaborative
- Directive
- Coaching

- Laissez faire

There are many leadership style questionnaires online to determine what kind of leader you are or, alternatively, you could hire a coach who will undertake them with you as part of a psychometric profiling session. This is not something to be scared of. It is about identifying your styles of behaviour so you can then play to your strengths and work on weaknesses or areas you're not strong in.

Little leaders. I love this. So often children are criticised and called bold in school, or they are labelled as trouble makers. In fact they are often leaders in waiting. I love the kids who do not adhere to the system. My son would always say what was on his mind. Teachers did not like that.

We received a call from my son's school principle He was eleven at the time. It was minor stuff as usual. She was so nice and so perfect and she asked to speak to Rory on the phone. My son's reply, at eleven years old, was tell her to "Go back to bitchville". A leader? Well he certainly did not conform. The children in school who stand out may have leadership potential and this should be greatly encouraged. Instead of telling them to sit down and effectively shut up we should be encouraging them to enter into dialogue.

We need to embrace and develop leadership skills. Public speaking and debating is an excellent way to develop these skills. It develops confidence for later in life and I think it is a vital tool. Do not rule out a quiet child from leadership duties. Leaders are not always the ones with the biggest mouths, often they are the quiet ones. Some of the best CEOs I know are very quiet and unassuming. They are silent but deadly. They are effective and get the job done nicely. "He who barks loudest often has the least to say". With children, give them every opportunity to grow into leadership. Give them every chance to develop their skills. Give them responsibility. Get them to organize others, to do tasks that requires leadership. Get them to be team captains. I always feel it is terrible in school teams when the best player is made captain. The role of captain should be shared. It is not always the best player who makes the best captain. The role of the leader captain is to pull the team together; it is about directing the team. Too often the leader wants all the glory. Rotating leaders is a good idea. I give people at every opportunity the chance to be a leader. When teaching, I get students to organize events themselves. When I am an employer, I ask my team to supervise, manage and deal with tasks. It empowers them and allows them to grow. How do we know what people are capable of until they try? Children are amazing leaders. Why? They have energy, vision, excitement, courage. They are fearless and treat everyone the same. They do not see things as black or white, as adults do. They see all people in the world as the same. Then we go to school and it is knocked out of us. We are told to conform. To do as we are told. A saying I often heard as a child was that "children should be seen and not heard". How awful. Expose them to everything. Take them to see you at work. Take them to everything that will help them grow, and trust them to make the right choices. I have often been amazed at the innate wisdom of children and teenagers. We think because they are young they do not know. Often they know more than we think, and often they are more wise than us. I remember once when I was not in a great space saying to my teenage son, "My life is a mess". His reply was that it was "Nothing that can't be fixed". I am so proud of those three wonderful children, now adults. (Well, two adults and a mini adult!) Allow people to be leaders, allow them to grow. More importantly, step up to the call yourself. Be an inspiration to others. Stand up for what is right. Do the right thing and make the world a better place. Everyone is a leader. The bin man, the janitor, the teacher, the artist. We are all leaders by the example we can set and by the role models we can be. Think about it! You do not need a title to be a leader. You just are own in the way you behave.

Task 33: How can I be a better leader?

What steps do I need to take to make me a better leader at home?
(List five ways:)

What steps do I need to take to make me a better leader at work?
(List five ways:)

What resources do I need to do this?

17. REGRET

Here are the regrets that some people getting had. Do not join them.

A nurse who looked after people in a palliative care environment said people told me they had the following regrets:

Firstly, people regretted not living a life true to themselves. Being what other people wanted them to be. They were not authentic. They wished they had honoured their dreams. Health is all you have and when you realise you do not have it anymore, it is too late. They regretted the choices they made. If they had made different choices, their life would have been different.

Secondly, they said they wished they had not worked so hard. Men said this. Almost each male client the nurse had looked after said they wished they had spent more time with their children, watching them grow up. Spent more time with their wife, instead of living life on the work treadmill. They deeply regretted this. Quite often, if you really look at your life and look at the income, you can make adjustments financially. Less money but more quality of life. Make it happen.

Thirdly, not expressing their true feelings. Those words left unsaid. Why can people not say what needs to be said? Imagine losing a loved one because you never had the courage to say, "I love you", or to say, "I am sorry, can you forgive me?" It is easier to get over ridicule than a lifetime of thinking about what could have been. Why did I not express my view, why did I not say what I needed to say? Why did I not say something at the time instead of repressing anger and resentment? Much illness today is due to repression. Depressed individuals who hold on to anger and hatred, often self-hate. Holding onto toxic emotions will kill you in the long term.

Fourthly, they said they wished they had been happier. They realised that happiness is a choice, and that they had a choice to be happy or not. It is like a coin. One side is happy with a happy face, the other is sad with a sad face. All you need to do is flip it over. You can choose to be happy!

Here are a few more to think about:

- Failing to keep fit and healthy. Only when you get old will you realise how fit you were before.
- Staying in a bad or abusive relationship.
- Not going to all those rock gigs. You are never too old.
- Not working harder in school. Wasting your to education. Again, it is never too late to go back to college.
- Not realizing how handsome, beautiful or wonderful you are. Everyone is beautiful and beauty is on the inside.
- Not listening to your parents. In contrast, as parents, not listening to your kids. Our youth are full of wisdom and knowledge. Listen!
- Not standing up for yourself. Not standing up to the bullies in school, work or home. Saying what

needs to be said, even if others disagree. It does not mean that they are right.

- Always forgive the person. You do not have to forgive the action, just the person.
- Caring too much about what other people think of you.
- Failing to finish what you start. Finish those projects!
- Failing to take risks, especially in love. Bigger risks have bigger pay offs.
- Worrying too much. Remember, "Worrying does not take away tomorrows troubles. It takes away today's peace".
- Not being grateful sooner. Say thank you and mean it. Remember the attitude of gratitude.
- Not asking that guy or girl out.
- Not buying that badass car! Personally I love this one.
- Not applying for my dream job.
- Not trying to work on or save my marriage.

The list is endless and perhaps it would give you some things to think about when you are looking at your goals. Have a look back at your goals from the earlier sections. Are they still important? Do they still matter?

18. Health and Fitness

If you are aiming to change your life and begin to shine, this chapter is really important. When you have done all the inner work, it is time to do all the outer work also. Looking good and feeling good. Life is all about balance, mental, physical and spiritual. Your health and fitness are vital.

What you eat, your exercise and your personal grooming routines are all really important. As Rihanna says, "Shine bright like a diamond."

Let's start with what you eat.

Your body is like a well-oiled machine. You are what you eat. It is amazing what people eat and think is good for them. Most of us have no dietary knowledge and food companies and advertisers fool us with fancy words when, really, you need to understand what you are really eating. What they class as healthy is often the opposite. An example of this is orange juice. We all drink some in the morning and think we are great. Typical orange cartons are full of sugar. So you get an instant sugar burst only to crash later. Real fresh oranges that are squeezed are way better for your body. Also, if you are having fruit for breakfast, do not have it alone. It is far too acidic for an empty stomach. Drink it with porridge or yogurt perhaps.

Sweet corn is something we all think is good for us but it actually produces a fat-storing chemical and is one of the things you should not eat if trying to lose body fat.

The food you put into your body is vitally important.

To start with, the most necessary nutrient of all is water. You can live without food but not water. All tissues and cells of the body need water. All the tissues and cells are bathed in water.

A healthy diet consists of a range of food types. The main types of food are grouped into the following:

- Fats
- Carbohydrates
- Proteins

The American Heart Association stated that women are more at risk of dying from heart disease than cancer or chronic lung disease. It pays to look after your heart. A well-balanced diet means just that: well balanced.

Look at the food pyramid on Google and review.

We should be eating foods from the base up, with very few sugars in our diet.

Fats:

The body needs fats for the following reasons:
We need a small amount of fat in our diets to provide essential fatty acids. Fatty acids are those fats that the body does not make itself. They are also needed to absorb fat soluble vitamins A, D, E and K – all of which

are required for healthy functioning of body systems. We require two types of essential fats, Omega 3 and Omega 6. Omega 3 is generally found in fish but also in small amounts in eggs, and spreads which include them. Omega 6 is found in vegetable oils, sunflower and spreads. We must be careful not to eat too much saturated fats. They are found in butter, cream, and some processed fat meats also found in cakes and pastries. Saturated fats can raise blood cholesterol and cause heart disease and strokes.

The following foods are high in fat and should be taken in moderation:

- Margarine, butter and other spreading fats.
- Cream
- Mayonnaise
- Cooking oils
- Salad dressings
- Fried food
- Chocolate, some crisps and biscuits
- Pastries, cakes, deserts and ice cream

How to cut down on fat:

- Choose spreads and oils high in polyunsaturated and monounsaturated fatty acids, such as rapeseed, olive, sunflower, soybean, safflower or flaxseed oil.
- If you use spreads, select ones that are lower/reduced fat for everyday use.
- Go for fruit scones instead of cakes and pastries.

- Avoid frying foods. Bake or grill and avoid putting butter on top.
- Choose fruit loaf or hot cross buns instead of croissants, pastries or cakes.

Be aware that if you eat any food, even if it is not high in fat, you need to burn it off or you may find the body stores it as a fat reserve. Hence the need to be active and get your exercise. It burns off fat! Exercise is vital not only for losing weight but because it helps all your internal organs to work better. The exercise needs to be regular and consistent. The harder you exercise the more calories you will burn.

Walking: Roughly 100 calories per mile are burned for a 180-pound person and 65 calories per mile for a 120-pound person. So if I weigh 9.5 stone, that is approximately 133 lbs, so if I walk one mile I lose 65 calories. Walking five miles would then burn off 300 calories. So if I eat one bar of average chocolate, I need to walk 5 miles. Cut out the sweets and chocolate and get walking.

Calories in chocolate *(Source: www.caloriecounting.co.uk):*

Dairy Milk, Cadbury's	1 Bar/49g	255
Dream, Cadbury's	1 Bar/45g	250
Rolo, Nestle	1 Pack/52.5 g	247
Dairy Milk with Caramel, Cadbury's	1 Bar/50g	240
Dairy Milk with Fruit & Nut, Cadbury's	1 Bar/49g	240
Toffee Crisp, Nestle	1 Bar/44g	227

Running burns more calories than walking because of the higher intensity. So if you can manage a higher intensity workout it is better for burning calories. Rowing is ideal, as it uses all muscle types.

Back to food!

Carbohydrates are what I call the fuel for the body. We need carbohydrates for energy. Carbohydrates are required for correct functioning of the immune system, blood clotting and human development.

High carb diets can lead to obesity, diabetes and cancer. Healthy sources of carbohydrates would be vegetables, beans, wholegrains, nuts and yogurt.

- Sugar is 100% pure carbs
- Breakfast cereal 91% pure carbs
- Cakes 79% pure carbs
- Jam 69% pure carbs

So you are really often eating pure sugar.

Do not be fooled by the manufacturers' alternative names for sugar. Sugar may also be known as sucrose, beet sugar, brown sugar, buttered syrup, cane-juice crystals, cane sugar, caramel, carob syrup, corn syrup solids, date sugar, dextran, dextrose, ethyl maltol and fructose.

Carbohydrates, or *saccharides,* are sugars and starches, which provide energy for the body.

There are two types of carbohydrates, **simple**, or *monosaccharides* and **complex**, or *polysaccharides.*

They are found in fruits and dairy products, and these simple carbohydrates are more easily digested by the body. The body breaks down simple carbs to be used for energy, which is used up very quickly. They are also often found in processed, refined foods such as white sugar, pastas, and white bread.

Another type of carbs, called complex carbohydrates, take longer for the body to digest and are most commonly found in vegetables (cellulose), whole grain breads and pasta, brown rice, and legumes.

Unrefined grains, like brown rice, retain the carbs whereas in the refining process of carbs the nutritional value is removed and the food loses its value. Therefore, quite often anything brown is better for you as it is not refined. For example, brown bread is better for you than white bread.

Eating a wholegrain cereal such as oatmeal will fill you up and give you longer lasting energy source than a bowl of sugar rich cereal which has little value. Porridge is a great cereal to start the day.

The liver digests carbohydrates by breaking them down into simple sugars better known as glucose. This in turn stimulates the production of insulin. The insulin provides energy to the cells of the body and will be used as energy.
Simple carbohydrates give that quick energy spike. For example eating, a chocolate bar, only to crash later. Whereas complex carbohydrates give a slower release and sustain a balanced blood sugar level.

The two different types of carbs affect the production of insulin differently—when digesting simple carbohydrates, insulin levels spike faster, and the carbs are used up more quickly for energy.

If the body produces too much glucose, it will be stored in the liver and muscle cells as glycogen, to be used for when the body needs an extra burst of energy. Any leftover glycogen that isn't stored in liver and muscle cells is stored as fat.

There is an important point here. If you eat too much of the simple carbohydrates and you do not exercise, they may not be burned off and may be stored in body fat. When trying to lose weight through exercise our body will resort to fat reserves and burn them off to get extra energy for the body.
The body uses the immediate store of glycogen for short bursts of exercise. For more strenuous exercise

or high intensity, the body uses its fat reserve as an energy source. The body can actually survive on proteins and fats alone. This would not be recommended long term and lack of carbs can result in muscle fatigue, cramps, and poor mental ability. All things in moderation! The normal recommended intake of carbs would be between 40% and 75% of our overall diet. Remember slow release carbs and remember that carbs are used for energy

.

Proteins:

Very important! They are needed for growth and development.

Proteins are required for DNA replication and metabolic activity. They are needed in the muscular system for the activity of muscles. Myosin and actin. Proteins are required for the immune system and many act as catalysts for change in body processes. They are broken down in digestion and used for metabolic actions. Your body needs different diets and food types depending on the stage you are in your life. For females, pregnancy and breast feeding bring there own dietary requirements. Diabetics also have special needs, as do people with allergies. Later in life as we get older our requirements change. There is loads of help and support out there. However I would recommend a professional (qualified) nutritional advisor. I often see slimming clubs and motivational groups and the person directing looks like they are unfit and not in great shape, which is not a good advertisement for health and fitness. They should look like a perfect reflection of health and people should aspire to be like them.

Vitamins and Minerals:

Your body needs a daily supply of vitamins and minerals to ensure optimum health levels. Here are some of the common vitamins required on a daily basis:

VITAMIN A
Growth and development. Good eyesight, healthy teeth and skin. Source – carrots.

VITAMIN B
Required for energy production, immune function, iron absorption and the general nervous system. Found in whole unprocessed foods, specifically whole grains, potatoes, bananas, lentils, chili peppers and beans.

VITAMIN C
Strengthens blood vessels and gives skin its elasticity, anti-oxidant function and iron absorption. Required for the immune system. Sources are oranges and other fruits and vegetables such as red and green peppers, kiwi, grapefruits, strawberries, Brussels sprouts.

VITAMIN D
Required for healthy teeth and bones. Sunshine helps in the stimulation of vitamin D. Vitamin D is also found in eggs and fish.

VITAMIN E
Required for healthy skin, blood circulation and protection from free radicals. (Free radicals are molecules which cause degeneration and aging of cells). Found in almonds and sunflower seeds as well as Avocado. Avocado is very good for skin.

VITAMIN K
Required for blood coagulation – that is, the process by which your blood clots. Found in greens, kale, spinach, Brussel sprouts and broccoli.

Minerals:

Folic acid:
Needed in pregnancy. Prevents birth defects. Helps People who are suffering from anemia. Broccoli, citrus fruits, peas, lentils, seeds and nuts. Supplements of folic acid are often given in pregnancy.

Calcium:
Required for healthy teeth and bones. Found in diary products, cheese, milk and yogurt.

Iron:
Good for muscles and healthy blood, especially in pregnancy, or for people who get heavy periods during menstruation. Found in Liver, oysters and soybeans, cereal, beans, lentils and spinach.

Zinc:

Required for a healthy immune system growth and fertility. Found in dark chocolate, spinach and cashew nuts.

As you can see it is vital to have a balance of all our nutrients, including fats, carbohydrates, proteins, vitamins and minerals. Many countries recommend the Mediterranean diet, as this diet is good for your heart. You can find A lot of information about this online but basically it follows the following guidelines.

Mediterranean Diet:

This is based on traditional food that countries surrounding the Mediterranean and is great for a health heart.

Eat plenty of vegetables and fruit daily, including potatoes, whole grain breads, cereals, pasta and rice, nuts and seeds.
Eat a little amount of cheese and yogurt low fat of course and eat fruit as a desert. Avoid butter and eat olive oil as your fat instead.
Weekly, have some fish and skinless poultry. Avoid red meats and eat only once or twice a month. Limit your intake of sweet items.

Reduce wine intake. Men: two glasses daily. Women: one. 5 oz glass.

There are some foods that are useful for losing weight as most of us are a few lbs over. Here is the list of some of those:

- Water (It flushes out toxins and hydrates. Often it will actually fill you up.)
- Green tea
- Grapefruit
- Apples and pears
- Oatmeal
- Broccoli
- Hot peppers
- Lean turkey
- Soups

With your diet, remember that you need to work off your food. So if you eat late in the evening and then sit for the night, your body is not burning off the calories. It is better to eat your main meal in the middle of the day, which gives you a few hours to burn it off. Do not drink stimulating drinks after 6pm as you may not sleep.

Alcohol is basically full of sugar and the calories are amazingly high. Alcohol is what they call empty calories. It has zero nutritional value.

Consider this:

Description	Serving Sizes	kCal	Fat(g)
Calories in Best/Premium Bitter	Pint	187	0
Calories in Draught Mild	Pint	136	0
Calories in Gin & Slimline Tonic	Single	56	0
Calories in Gin & Tonic	Single	120	0
Calories in Red Wine	175ml Glass	119	0
Calories in Regular Bitter	Pint	170	0
Calories in Regular Dry Cider	Pint	204	0
Calories in Vodka & Coke	175ml	120	0
Calories in Vodka & Diet Coke	Single	56	0
Calories in Vodka, Lime & Soda	200ml	76	0
Calories in Whisky & Lemonade	175ml	82	0
Calories in White Wine - Dry	175ml Glass	116	0
Calories in White Wine Spritzer (lemonade)	225ml	138	0

So, ladies, if you drink two of wine glasses a night that is 232 calories x 7 = 1,624 calories. That means you need to do five x five mile runs to burn that off!

Task 34: Diet Plan

Examine your current eating habits. Review and make changes. Keep a food log for one week if unsure. Ask the following questions:

What is my current weight?
Is this within the healthy range?
Does this need to change?

Your log should contain the following:

Foods I need to avoid:
Things that will be good for me:
Water intake:
My dietary goal:

Physical exercise:

Your body works best when it is holistically tuned through both mental and physical fitness. You cannot have one without the other. There are mental exercises you can do to keep your mind in top shape and they are vital. But you must also ensure to get physically fit.

When we undertake exercise, we produce endorphins. These are happy hormones that make us feel good. Hence if you go to the gym in a bad mood chances are you will feel great when you leave and the bad mood has vanished. Believe me! Exercise does the following:

It gets your metabolism going. It gets the blood flowing around the body. This is vital for all normal body functions to work. All organs and tissues of the body need clean blood to work and also to remove waste. So, each time you exercise, you bring clean blood to the areas and it also speeds up removal of waste via the lymphatics and the venous system. It helps us to burn off calories and gets the heart pumping. When you sit at your desk all day and get no exercise, smoke, eat cheeseburgers and drink five pints a night, your body gets sluggish and over-loaded with toxins. Your body is like a set of motorways all congested and blocked with the nutrients not getting to where they need to go. The best time to exercise is first thing in the morning as it gets the metabolism going. But not for everyone. I find my blood sugar not great in the morning and so I run better later in the day when I have more sugar in me.

Good sugar, not six mars bars! You can also get sugar from fruit.

Some facts about exercise:

Exercise can help you lose weight as it helps to burn calories. Small steps, even taking the stairs instead of taking the lift, can be of benefit.

Exercise can help reduce other health conditions, such as high blood pressure, high cholesterol, diabetes or the risk of stroke, cardio vascular conditions and depression.

When getting fit and taking regular exercise, you feel good about yourself as you are doing something positive for your inner body as well as your outer image.

People say they are too tired to exercise but exercise actually gives you energy. Sometimes you are far too tired to go to the gym and by the time you are finished you are ready for round two. Bring it on. Your body actually starts to crave it. You can become addicted to the adrenalin and the good endorphins, so remember: everything in moderation! But great to be addicted to exercise. Your body will crave it eventually and it will become part of your everyday life and your routine.

They say that running is meditation in motion. I always feel better after a run. When starting any kind of exercise, if in doubt of your medical condition, always check with a doctor first and or a fitness instructor. I would only consult a professional who looks fit themselves.

Fitness resolutions:

To keep you motivated and keep your eye on the target you need to have a very clear plan and to stay focused and motivated.

Here are some tips:

Make a commitment to living a fitter and healthy life. What does that actually mean to you? Commit – write it down.

I, Clodagh Swanson, on this day 23rd of November am committing myself to living a healthy and more positive life.

Date it and sign it.

Remember the tone of the language used could be your downfall. If you say to yourself I am going to lose weight you are instantly in your mind LOSING. You subconsciously feel at a loss. Instead if you should reframe it as a gain.

I am gaining a better lifestyle and a fitter body. It is more positive in its approach. I am gaining vitality and health. Do not say you are losing – you are not, you're gaining.

Keep it simple and do not make too many resolutions as too many goals could mean that your individual goals do not get enough focus. Few goals and more focus.

Slow and steady wins the race, so pace yourself. You probably cannot get up today and say I will run 5k or 10k right now. If you are not used to running, start with a run/walk structure for your plan.

If you try to do too much, you will lose motivation and give up. Keep the end in mind and visualize the "new" you: radiant, wonderful and fit. We are not talking about getting the body of a body builder. We are talking about a healthy and fit body.

Keep the chin up and keep yourself motivated. When you feel like giving up, phone a motivational buddy. I call or text a coach buddy and tell them how I feel, and they will tell me to keep pushing forward. And remember that pain is temporary, it always goes away.

Do a weekly schedule and allocate the times and the dates for your exercise, otherwise the week is gone and you have nothing done. You need to prioritise this.

The different types of exercise:

Endurance:
Also known as 'aerobic', these activities increase your breathing and heart rate. They keep your heart, lungs, and circulatory system healthy and improve your overall fitness. Building your endurance makes it easier to carry out many of your everyday activities. A good brisk walk, jogging or a run would do.

Strength:
This is making your muscles stronger. These exercises also are called "strength training" or "resistance

training." Examples include:

- Lifting weights
- Using a resistance band
- Using your own body weight

Balance
Helps prevent falls, a common problem in older adults. Many lower-body strength exercises also will improve your balance. Tai Chi is brilliant for improving balance.

Flexibility
Stretches your muscles and can help your body stay limber. Being flexible gives you more freedom of movement.

Aerobic exercise
Also known as **cardio**, this is physical exercise of low to high intensity. Some examples of this are long distance running, jogging, cycling and swimming. Anaerobic exercise is different in that it is mainly strength training and short distance running. The use of energy in the body is different.

Action 34: What new exercise methods will I take on board?

List these daily:

List these weekly:

Who can I ask for help?

What is my overall fitness goal?

Remember! Sign and commit!

Personal grooming. The icing on the cake:

Why is this so important when looking at your life? It takes 20 seconds to make an impression. When someone meets you for the first time, this is what they base their impressions on.

First impressions are broken down into:

7% – What you say
38% – Your body language
55% – How you look

It is vital to send the right message! You need to look smart, presentable and project an image of confidence. It is vital to success. Research in the US showed that women who were professionally groomed, with make-up (not over the top make-up) were paid more and got promoted quicker. For men, it is no different. You are the message.

So how do you project the correct image? Well, let's break it down.

Personal grooming. We will now talk about skincare, wardrobe planning and body language. It is vital. Imagine you are going for an interview or a very important business meeting. You need to immediately present a good impression. You are the message.

Grooming. Is your hair tidy? If you're a lady, it should be professionally turned out. No roots showing and tossed messed hair. No cheap hair grips or hair accessories – it looks unprofessional. Ensure it is not greasy. Same for the gentleman.

Next the skin. Your skin is the largest organ in the body. Its main function is to form a framework for the skeletal system holding our bones together and it also protects the acid mantle. What the acid mantle does is that it forms a protective layer of sebum and sweat on the skin. It protects the skin from bacterial infection and from the environment. When this is stripped, you have a skin that reacts and results in breakouts and redness flaky areas or dehydration. It is not water dry, it is oily dry. There is a big difference. To help keep your skin and you looking young, you need to drink at least three litres of water per day. Yes, that is the boys too. You men need to mind your skin more than us ladies, as you are shaving and often working out in the elements.

Protecting your skin and the acid mantle is vital. Otherwise the skin gets old looking and lined. When it gets dry, it either a lack of water or oil or both. Knowing your skin type is vital. If you use the wrong products and follow the wrong skin care routine, you will do more damage than you would if you used nothing at all. I have spent years looking at skin as a therapist in my beauty days and a huge amount of clients and young girls were using incorrect products, thinking they are doing the right thing and actually making their skin worse. Often using things like facial washes and alcohol-based toners strip the skin, resulting in angry inflammation.

The skin's natural lubricant is sebum and it is needed to maintain a healthy skin. Strip it and the skin gets lined. That is why an oily skin never looks as old as dry skin. Another point to consider is the damage smoking does to the skin. It starves the skin of oxygen and nutrients. This resulting in dry, lined, old skin. It also takes on a grey appearance.

Skin types:

<u>Dry Skin</u>
Dry skin is either lacking water or oil. It may look pale or transparent. Fine lines may be evident. There may be milia around the eyes. (Milia are little white spots, which may be hard as a rock under the skin and around the eye area.) They can be massaged gently to try to disperse the sebum trapped underneath the skin. Drink three litres of water a day. Use cleansers that are oil based, which means there is more oil in them than water. A good example would be p Ponds cold creams. Cream cleansers are better for a dry skin. Use a toner that is alcohol free and use a rich day-and-night cream. You need a night cream to be richer as we lose more water at night. Dry skin needs to have an emollient effect on the skin, which means it will trap water in the skin and retain water. Most people do not know what a moisturiser does. It does not put moisture into the skin. It prevents moisture from getting out. Sorry people, paying €300 for a product does not mean it works. Eat plenty of fish and nuts, and avocados. Natural home-made products can be excellent. Astral, Nivea and the likes are certainly fine. I have used a wide range of cosmetic products and they are great, but remember that quite often you

are paying for packaging.

Oily Skin

The sebaceous glands are producing a lot of oil. This is required to maintain the acid mantle but careful attention needs to be paid to oily skin as it can present many skin problems for both adults and young people. Oily skin often has a sallow appearance. Less lines. Blocked pores can emerge, though not always. Blocked pores are not dirt! They appear when oil is trapped. If the oil is trapped under the skin and the skin is covering the opening onto the surface, then you get a white head. When the sebum comes to the surface and there is are no blocked pores you get a black head as it oxidises. Strict facial hygiene is necessary to avoid large blocked pores getting infected or in some cases developing into sebaceous cysts. Oily skin needs a facial cleanser with a water base not oil base. You would likely need a toner which is astringent, and which will take the oil away, but not overly strong. If it is too strong it can take too much oil away and you will be left with striped skin, 'sensitized' skin, or you may get irritated, reactive skin, which would be quite red and dry. Most facial washes do this and they are not really a good idea. Listen to this, Moms! A lot of the facial washes for teens are terrible, and can make the problem worse. Take those boys and girls to a reputable skin care clinic or salon and have their skin diagnosed. Dermalogica are good as all their therapists should be trained well. Remember though, wrong products can result in very damaged skin.

Combination Skin

Quite common is dry and sensitive. This means you have dry areas and sensitive areas on one face. Often this might mean sensitive cheeks with broken capillaries and redness, possibly from using the wrong products, or from extremes of heat and cold. For a combination skin use a product for the most important issue. If it is dry sensitive I would suggest a product for sensitive skin for general use, together with a really good moisturiser for night-time.

Mature skin

This is really any skin over the age of 24. Skin needs to be really well looked after. Anti-aging products are everywhere, but we cannot stop aging. The main cause of fine lines and deep lines come from things like smoking and dehydration. Three litres of water a day are vital and you should also ensure your moisturiser is emollient-based, which prevents moisture loss.

I will not go into all the skin conditions and disorders but what I would say is that when you are young you have the skin you were born with, and when you are older you have the skin you deserve.

Male skin care:

You really need to cleanse and tone just like the ladies. However, again, ensure you use the right products. Most male products are generic and do not come in a range of skin types. Again I would advise actually going to a salon to purchase products. They will do a skin analysis and tell you what you should be using. A facial scrub can be good for trapped hairs and blocked follicles so use those wonderful therapists and get good advice. A hot towel shave is a must for guys who want soft, supple, fantastic skin. I can tell instantly if a guy has had a hot towel shave because their skin looks great!

Personal grooming products

Cleansers come in all skin types used for cleaning the skin. Toner will remove the last traces of makeup and cleanser, leaving the skin fresh and the pores tightened.

Moisturiser will prevent moisture loss from the skin. It cannot put moisture in. Some have better ingredients than others. Collagen and elastin are good to have in the product. Avoid ingredients such as lanolin or retinol as they are can cause allergic reactions in some people.

Eye creams are useful but often a cheap one is as good if not better than an expensive one. Our science teacher in beauty college told us that Vaseline is the best moisturiser on the market as no water can get through it. If you retain water or have puffy eyes, I would not use an eye cream as it can make the matter worse.

Salon treatments:

A good facial should be done every few months and will really benefit the skin. A facial should include the following:

- A double cleanse
- Toning
- Steaming
- A facial peel
- Massage to the face neck and shoulders
- Moisturiser

Other types of facial are available, such as electrical facials. Your salon will advise as to what you might try. The routine is great to deep cleanse the skin as at home we are normally in a rush and only do a quick cleanse.

Make-up products:

Make-up should be applied using the correct type of product for the correct skin type. Men, if very pale, can use a tinted moisturiser. Again, for the ladies, be careful with your purchase of product. A dry skin should use a make-up with more oil in it and an oily skin should use a product with more water in it.
  All make-ups, liquids and creams should be set with a translucent powder to avoid cracking of the makeup and to help it set. Make-up will last longer if done correctly. Cheeks should have a hint of blusher in a colour that matches the client's skin tone. Two tones are usually found, warm and cool. If you're a warm skin tone, your make-up will have yellow in it and if you are a cool skin tone it will have pink in it.
  "Milk and roses versus peaches and cream".

The same goes for your eye cosmetics. If cool, use cool colours, if warm use warm.

Mascara should be black or brown depending, again, on your colouring. A professional colour analysis session can guide you on this. I used to do colour analysis and it is amazing how the wrong colours can appear to add 15 lbs body weight to a person. Also, for most people, black is a no-no. It should only be worn near the face on 'winter' colour types. It makes you look tired and will result in you having dark circles under the eyes.

Wardrobe planning:

I love this. It is so wise to have a style consultation done, and this applies to both men and women. Identify what type of body shape you have. Are you tall, straight or curved? It is important, as clothes will fit you better and look better if they are for your correct body shape. I joke not.

A simple style trick for women (and men) would be to never stop a line at the widest part of your body. Always have it at the slimmest. So, for ladies skirts if you have a heavy calf, the skirt should stop above the knee or below the calf. Otherwise it draws attention to it.

It is important to plan and build a wardrobe "capsule", that costs very little and is highly versatile. Spend your money where you spend your time. If you work in a chic city office, most of your clothes will be for work. If you're a mum who does not work, it might be more casual. If you're consistently attending functions, this is where your money will be spent. There is also a rule about cost per wear. An item of clothing is only expensive if you do not wear it. For example, if a man buys a suit for €500 this is the cost per wear:

Suit cost €500	Worn 3 times per week	3 x 52 = 156	500/156 = €3.20 each time worn
Suit cost €300	Only worn 2 times	2	Cost per wear €150.00
Watch €600	Worn every day for 3 years	3 x 365 =	Cost per wear €0.54

Get the idea? So it is often better to purchase a better quality item, as you may get more time out of it, for example, a good leather bag or briefcase.

Putting it all together:

Start at the top. Ensure hair and facial grooming is well prepared and in top shape.

Next, oral hygiene is vital. Bad breath or poor dental care can let you down. It is quite easy not to have dental work done. Travel abroad and get veneers if your teeth are letting you down. A smile is the greatest asset you have. Wear it always. It is contagious.

Next plan your outfit and ensure everything matches or co-ordinates well. Remember you have only 20 seconds to make an impression.

Ladies, tights or stockings are a must for a professional image at work. Bare legs are not professional. Gentlemen, make sure your socks match and, more importantly, your shoes! It does happen. Believe me. Sitting in a meeting with odd shoes has happened before.

Also ensure that your shoes are polished and in good repair. And, of course, no smelly feet!

When all that is done, you will be ready for action. You're looking good!

Female wardrobe essentials:

10 -12 items will give you 15 outfits.
Select color combinations that suit your color palette.
Have a professional color consultation done.
Use neutrals as the basis for your wardrobe.

If you are a dark or deep colouring – like Elizabeth Taylor or Oprah – then black would be your basic colour to work with. Trousers and dresses, skirts and so on. Your shirts would be a crisp white. You can add splashes of colour, such as red, purple, royal blue etc.

For a more autumnal colouring, your basics may be navy or deep brown. Only the winter personality should wear black close to the face. Autumn neutrals would be browns, navy and blouses would be a cream or off white.

A light summer look, like Lady Diana, would be neutrals of navy for suits and work wear. White shirts works well as a summer looks will work in all the cool colors, like blues, pinks, lavender and all the pastel colours.

Our spring person can be a mass of colour, bright, with a bright eye. Neutrals would be navy.

For a working woman, your wardrobe include:

Two/three jackets – different colours
Three skirts or slacks in different colours and one in a dark navy or black
Three shirts
A dress
Some extra tops, perhaps one or two slim fit knitwear. They can be worn to work or with casual clothes.

For off duty time, have a couple of pairs of good jeans and jumpers to mix and match. You might have a good pair of dressy chino type slacks to wear with a crisp white blouse, and throw a jumper around the neck.

Shoes:

Keep your main selection to the basics.

Two pairs for work in a neutral color and one or two evening pairs again in neutral colors to match all outfits.

Walking shoes and trainers for your exercise class. Do not go to the gym looking like you have no style. Buy some lovely fitness gear.
A range of accessories such as necklaces and a good watch are vital. A classy watch is all you need for the business world.
A good quality leather bag, briefcase and belt. Accessories need to be avoided for business, unless you are running a fashion empire.
Ensure you have a nice, good quality pen, not bitten or chewed and a filo fax is a good idea. Create a professional image.

For the gentlemen:

Spend your money where you spend your time.

If working in an office I would suggest two good suits. Buy a good one that fits you correctly. No short trousers or sleeves that are too long. Pinstripes slim a fuller rounder body shape, either with shirts or slacks. Do not wear jumpers with horizontal lines as they will make you look bigger. If you are carrying a few pounds extra, avoid all fabrics which are bulky as they will add bulk to you.
   Crisp white shirts are always a good idea but ensure they really are white. So many men wear a white shirt that is 100 years old and it is no longer actually white. Again, you guys can have your colours done. Pick some lovely pastel shades, like pink, lavender or crisp blue. It can bring some colour to your face so you do not look like John Major. Always wear a good leather

belt and good quality, trendy shoes. Ensure they are polished and that they match, and that your socks do too. For boys, a range of trouser and shirts, together with a couple of jackets would be a good idea. Single breasted works best if you're large.

For both males and females, a good coat in a neutral colour is important. Accessories for the guys could include nice cufflinks and a classic watch. Some nice jeans and well co-ordinated shirts and jumpers can work for the casual times. For the gym, please smarten up boys!

And that is it, really. There are some really good books out there for style and wardrobe planning, but remember, the prettiest thing you can wear or the handsomest thing you can wear is a smile.

You're looking good. Now you're shining inside and outside.

19. Your best life

Well, you have done a lot of inner work and outer work. I guess your shining by now. So let's do our final task!

Task 36: Create your bucket list

The bucket list:

What is your bucket list? This is a list of all the things you would like to do before you kick the bucket. Remember, your life is like a jar of coffee. You only have a certain number of granules. The granules are days. Once that coffee jar starts to empty you cannot fill the jar of life up again. Each day is precious and you will never get it back. You must use your time wisely. It is a valuable commodity. Do not waste a single grain. And do not give your time to useless things like self-pity and regret. Use your time for the good. What will you add to your bucket list? Ask yourself the following questions:

- What have you always wanted to do but have not done yet?
- What countries, places do you want to visit?
- What are your biggest goals and dreams?
- What are they key achievements you want to achieve?

- What experiences do you want to have?
- What new things do you want to experience?
- What new skills do you want to learn or try?
- What legacy do you want to leave for the world?
- What do you want to be remembered for?
- When your gone what do you want people to say about you?
- Are there any special moments you want to witness?
- What are the most important things you can ever do?
- Are there any specific people you want to meet in person?
- What do you need to do to lead a life of the greatest meaning?
- What can you do in your community to make the world a better place?
- What things need to be said before it is too late?

People say, "Oh sure I do not have the money to do that, I could never afford that". They have not event tried. Some of the most beautiful experiences in life are free.

- Watching a sunrise or sunset.
- Watching the tide rush in or the waves crash against the rocks.
- Helping someone else to be successful.
- Doing a few random acts of kindness for someone who may need your help.
- Helping someone by just actually listening.

- Walking 10K on a sunny day. Because it is something you would rather not do. If you're lazy stretch yourself.

They say do something every day you do not actually want to do. Perhaps something that is good for you, like a walk, exercise or a healthy meal.
When you are compiling your list make sure you have some of the following headings:

- Fun
- Adventure
- Community
- Health and fitness
- Travel
- Friends
- Work or career
- Training and education
- Helping others
- Nature
- Financial
- Family
- Sport

The list is endless. You might want to swim with dolphins, hot air balloon, parachute jump. Maybe you want to fly a plane, travel to Africa, work in an orphanage or do good deeds. Maybe you'd like to get a tattoo. It is your bucket list. Your life. Ensure it is fun. Stick pictures up of the things you want to do.

Sadly now I must leave you. I hope you have enjoyed this journey of exploration and awareness. I am sure for some there was a tear, or for others you did not gel with the content. That is ok too. For me, I hope it will help a few fellow travellers to join me.

I may be contacted by email should you have any requests for help or need any advice. We are now friends.

I hope life will be kind to you on your forward path. Remember, be kind, be honest and always do your best you can do no more. And, remember too, the world is a better place because you are in it.

Clodagh

xxx

Tips for life:

- Smile
- Laugh
- Listen
- Perform random acts of kindness
- Tell someone you love them everyday
- Compliment others every time you can
- Spent time in nature
- Do something you do not want to do, that will make you grow as a person
- Hug people as often as possible
- Call your Mum
- Call your Dad
- Tell your children you're proud of them
- Tell your team you're proud of them
- Tell your employees you're proud of them
- Climb a mountain
- Learn new skills
- Learn to say no sometimes
- Learn to say yes to yourself
- Treat yourself to good food
- Exercise daily
- Talk to God
- Wear nice underwear and sparkle from within
- Buy the bad ass car
- Holiday
- Save some money and spent the rest
- Send someone flowers

- Help your community
- Talk to old people they have a lot of wisdom
- Educate yourself daily
- Read inspirational books
- Get rid of your TV
- Do something to help the homeless
- Do something to help the youth
- Work more efficiently and not longer
- Take time off
- Mind your mental and physical health
- Sleep – but not too much
- Dance
- Spend time at the ocean
- Love your self
- Respect others
- Be a person of integrity
- Inspire others
- Find your passions
- Do a job you love
- Find your true vocation
- Follow your heart
- Dream big
- Help others achieve their dreams
- Be kind

Quotes on Failure:

"This is courage to bear unflinchingly what heaven sends." (Euripides)

"Those who have gone through the door have completed half their journey."
(Italian Proverb)

"Our prayers are answered not when we are given what we ask, but when we are challenged to be what we can be." (Morris Achller)

"Do not wait to strike until the iron is hot; but make it hot by striking" (William B. Sprague)

"My will shall shape my future. Whether I fail or succeed shall be no man's doing but my own. I am the force. I can clear any obstacle before me or I can be lost in the maze. My choice, my responsibility: Win or lose, only I hold the key to my destiny." (Elaine Maxwell)

"Hard work pays of in the future, ease pays off now." (Anon.)

"Success is twenty years of hard work to become an overnight success" (Anon.)

"Be like a postage stamp, stick with it until you get there." (Harvey Mackey)

Quotes on goals:

"To realise ones destiny is a person's only real obligation." (Paulo Coehlo)

"In life as in football you won't go far unless you know where the goalposts are." (Arnold H Glasgow)

"Nothing great in this world was achieved without enthusiasm."
(Emerson)

"Who said it could not be done? And what great victories has he to his credit which qualify him to judge others accurately?" (Napoleon Hill)

"When defeat comes, accept it as a signal that your plans are not sound, rebuild those plans, and set sail once more toward your coveted goal." (Napoleon Hill)

"Action is the real measure of intelligence". (Anon.)

"All achievements, all earned riches, have their beginning in an idea." (Napoleon Hill)

"All the breaks you need in life wait within your imagination. Imagination is the workshop of your mind, turning mind energy into accomplishment and wealth." (Napoleon Hill)

"Any idea, plan, or purpose may be placed in the mind, through repletion of thought." (Napoleon Hill)

"Effort only fully releases its reward after a person refuses to quit." (Napoleon Hill.)

"Every adversity, every failure, every heartache comes with it the seed of an equal or greater benefit." (Napoleon Hill)

"Great achievement is born of great sacrifice, and is never the result of selfishness." (Napoleon Hill)

"The most interesting thing about a postage stamp is the persistence to which it sticks to its job." (Napoleon Hill)

"When your desires are strong enough you will appear to possess superhuman powers to achieve." (Napoleon Hill)

"A pessimist sees the difficulty in every opportunity, an optimist sees the opportunity in every difficulty." (Winston Churchill)

"You have enemies? Good. That means you have stood up for something in your life." (Winston Churchill)

"I never worry about action, only inaction." (Winston Churchill)

"If you are going through hell, keep going." (Winston Churchill)

"Failure is a delay but not defeat. It is a temporary detour, not a dead end street." (William Arthur Ward)

"Time is a master worker that heals the wounds of temporary defeat, and equalises the inequalities and rights the wrongs of the world. There is nothing impossible with time." (Napoleon Hill)

"Most people have attained their greatest successes just one step beyond their greatest failure." (Napoleon Hill)

"No man can succeed in a line of endeavour which he does not like." (Napoleon Hill)

"No man ever achieved worthwhile success who did not, at one time or another find himself at least one foot hanging well over the brink of failure." (Napoleon Hill)

"When a web is begun, God gives the thread." (Inscribed on the ceiling of the Library of Congress)

"If you will be clearly what you are, the universe will give you clearly what you want." (Abraham Hicks)

"Men succeed when they realise that their failures are the preparation for their victory." (Ralph Waldo

Emerson)

"Leap and the net will appear." (Julia Cameron)

"Problems are to the mind what exercise is to the muscle, they toughen and make strong." (Norman Vincent Peal)

Quotes on Fear:

"Fear is a dark room where negatives are made." (Anon.)

"Fears are nothing more than a state of mind." (Anon.)

"Thinking will not overcome fear but action will." (W Clement Stone)

"So many fail because they don't get started. They don't go. They fail to begin." (W Clement Stone)

"If the creator had a purpose in equipping us with a neck, he surely would meant us to stick it out." (Arthur Koestler)

Made in the USA
Middletown, DE
27 July 2017